Christmas and the Mark of the Beast

(A Spiritual Teaching for the Body of Christ)

Rev 20:4
4 And I saw thrones, and they sat upon them, and judgment was given unto them: and I saw the souls of them that were beheaded for the witness of Jesus, and for the word of God, and which had not worshipped the beast, neither his image , neither had received his mark upon their foreheads, or in their hands; and they lived and reigned with Christ a thousand years.
KJV

Biblical
TEACHER

Samuel Williams

Christmas and the Mark of the Beast
(A Spiritual Teaching for the Body of Christ)

Samuel Williams

To order additional copies, visit,
www.createspace.com/ 8142658
Facebook page: Christmas and the Mark of the Beast
http://samuelkem.wixsite.com/truthaboutthetithe
Contact the author via email at samuelkem@aol.com.

Printed by Createspace an Amazon.com company
Printed in the United States of America 2018
First Edition

Acknowledgements

When we meet God, it will be on His terms and not ours!

I dedicated this book to Brother Blaize, the first person I witnessed teaching His family the truth about Christmas. You were the first example of a man of God in my life. Thank you for being a role model that walked in the truth. Thank you for being a true man of God that was an example to me in my youth. May the blessings of the Lord continue to overtake you.

This book is also dedicated to all those who have been ridiculed for taking a stance against Christmas. For those who knew something was wrong but were unable to articulate their feelings to others because of a lack of knowledge. For those who have felt a shift every Christmas season as if God was reaching through the fog to get their attention. To those who believe there is no proof in scripture that Christmas is not of God. For those pastors and ministers who have come to the realization that this holiday is not ordained by God but felt intimidated to bring the fullness of the truth to their congregation. To those heaven-bent on making it into the Kingdom. This book is for all of you. Be blessed.

Contents

Foreword

It was December 1987. I was home from Germany not quite six months, honorably discharged after finishing my commitment to the armed services. Back home in good ole Miami, The Temperature was cooling down and we were entering my favorite time of the year. It was close to winter and my favorite holiday even though I was not a believer. It was the Christmas season and you could feel the spirit in the air. Decorated storefronts, Christmas trees everywhere, and houses lit up in the night. My hometown radio station WEDR was blasting Christmas songs 24/7. I loved Christmas. Eggnog, parties, gifts, liquor, love, and everyone is happy at Christmas time. Yep, this was going to be a good Christmas.

Metaphorically speaking, the brakes of the car shrieked as the whole Christmas season came to a full stop. My parents called me over to the house to let me know they no longer celebrated Christmas. They tried to explain how Christmas actually had nothing to do with Christ. I wasn't having it. No one was going to ruin my Christmas even though I was not a believer. My parents did not know that I had turned my back on the Bible. I wasn't about to announce it to them. Even though I grew up in the church this was the time of my life that I rejected God for science. Funny, I didn't believe yet I swore no one was going to take my Christmas away without a fight. The fact that I, an unbeliever, who had not yet come to Christ was hell-bent on enjoying Christmas should have shined the light on the truth if I was paying attention, but I wasn't. I headed to the local library to prove to my parents that Christmas was as much a part of Christianity as Christ. Wow was I in for a shock.

I grew up going to church but as I got to the end of my teenage years, I started asking questions that no one in the church could answer. I was being bombarded in school with science and evolution and I had not yet realized that school was actually a propaganda tool whose source was the world kingdom and Satan.

I asked a deacon if the world was round or flat and he told me according to the Bible it was flat. That pretty much sealed it. The nail in the coffin was trying to read and understand the book Revelation. The attempt ended with the Bible being thrown into a drawer and me stating, "These people crazy." It is funny how things come full circle because today I am the one being asked those questions. I can show people in the Bible that the world is a sphere, and much of the sealed book of Revelation, God in His mercy has unsealed to me so I can teach it. I love being a teacher in the Body of Christ because I wish when I had all my questions, there would have been someone available to give me the right answers.

As I look back at my school days, I can also see that God was already preparing me to teach the Body of Christ. I had this pull to read as much as I could about mythology. I had little interest in reading but if it was comic books or mythology, then I could do it. I was interested in every legend and myth. Maybe this is why I fell in love with J.R. Tolkien's books the Hobbit, and Lord of the Rings, which had a mythological style to them. As a teacher for the Kingdom, I now understand the draw of witchcraft that is in these types of books and can warn young people to avoid them. I can effectively teach on these matters because God has used what I learned to shine the light on the devices of the enemy.

As I started doing my research, I realized that Christmas was definitely linked to myths and legends. I was seeing the patterns, remembering the stories, and could see how the rituals tied to sources outside the Bible. I was finding the traditions practiced for Christmas everywhere. The Bible only mentioned these traditions in a negative sense. Many of the traditions were already being utilized in pagan religions long before Christ came as the Lamb of God. The celebration of His birthday, other than the initial proclamation of His birth, is nowhere in scripture. Three hundred years had passed before the annual celebrations even started.

There I was sitting in the library with all these books open and I could not find anything to help me win my argument. Everything gave support to the truth of what my parents were telling me. Yet little did I realize that many years later the Holy Spirit would take me on this search again. Although I thought I had uncovered tons of evidence to show Christmas did not originate from Christianity, what the Holy Spirit revealed to me made me realize what I learned as an unbeliever was a drop in the bucket. It could not compare to what God would show me after I received the baptism of the Holy Spirit.

I was empowered in my vocation as a teacher in the Body of Christ. It is a whole other level when you surrender to God and put your trust in Him to teach you. Who teaches like God? What I am about to share is the truth but I do apologize for the hurt I am about to cause many. However, I see no way around it. This knowledge is about to ruin your Christmas and at the same time greatly increase your chances of making it into the kingdom. Take a deep breath and let's get started.

Christmas and the Mark of the Beast

Introduction

It has been more than 30 years since I did my research on Christmas as a non-believer. God has brought me a long way. I truly had no idea how deep this well of knowledge would go. What I have learned about Christmas history and the grip it has on the world has truly been amazing. I thought it was just a holiday but over the years, I have learned that the whole world has been fooled. What you are going to learn about Christmas and how it is tied to the mark of the beast is going to be shocking. Yes, this is going to ruin your Christmas but in a good way because your chances of eternal life will increase dramatically. This will not be a feel-good teaching. The information is going to make you ponder the very content of your belief. Many will start to understand how diabolical the fight against our souls really is and how we need to evaluate all that we accept as truth, with in-depth study.

The enemy has always been good at deflecting the truth that exposes his modes of operation. I understand how strong the fight will be against this truth on Christmas. I have been called a false prophet, false teacher, and accused of teaching doctrines of devils on many occasions while trying to shine the light of truth on Christmas. I have been fighting this battle too long but I am undaunted.

One of the low points in this journey to expose the truth was when a close friend said that I was teaching doctrines of devils after I shared with him what God was showing me about Christmas. I had to bite my tongue but I will admit it hurt because this came from someone who was very close to me. We had many days of fellowshipping together and I considered him a trusted friend. Yet his words cut like a knife and cut deeply. I walked away and did not respond.

God was teaching me at this time in my life that the revelations He was exposing me to in scripture, would not be accepted by many initially. I would give the word and be rejected and discouraged to the point where I did not want to speak the things God was showing me. God quickly let me know that I was not the first person with this complaint. He had me read Jeremiah's complaint.

Jer 20:7-9

7 O LORD, thou hast deceived me, and I was deceived: thou art stronger than I, and hast prevailed: I am in derision daily, every one mocketh me.

8 For since I spake, I cried out, I cried violence and spoil; because **the word of the LORD was made a reproach unto me, and a derision, daily.**

9 Then I said, I will not make mention of him, nor speak any more in his name. But his word was in mine heart as a burning fire shut up in my bones, and I was weary with forbearing, and I could not stay.

KJV

Jeremiah was distraught because of the opposition he was getting from the very people God was sending him to speak to. He decided he would not speak the Word of God. Yet the word became like fire in his heart as if enclosed in his very bones and he was forced to release (speak) it before it consumed him. He had no choice but to speak.

Like Jeremiah, I decided I would continue to speak because to hold in what God was showing me caused more suffering than speaking the truth. God reassured and taught me that my job was just to drop the seed of the Word in the heart of the person and go on my way. He would have it watered and if the person was receptive to the living water, then the seed would grow and produce fruit. Who teaches like God?

Months after I spoke to my friend on the truth about Christmas, God gave me a powerful revelation on how mango trees have to go through a period of hardship to produce fruit. If they do not have a dry season, then they will not blossom and produce mangoes. God showed me how as believers we have to go through the same thing. We go through periods of trails and tribulations (dry seasons) but the end result is that we blossom and produce fruit. I shared this with a group of co-workers as we gathered for our weekly prayer after work. The same friend that had accused me of false doctrine and doctrines of devils concerning what I taught on Christmas was in the group and was blown away by the revelation. He could not stop talking about the truth he received and what a blessing it was to him.

We all held hands and I started to lead the group in prayer. In the middle of my prayer, I had the strange feeling come over me to open my eyes and look in front of me. When I did, I observed the same friend looking shocked and shaken to the point that he had to lean back on one of the cars in the parking lot where we were praying.

After I finished the prayer, I asked him, "What was wrong?" He said, "God just spoke to me." I asked him, "What did He say?" He answered, "What Samuel just told you was the truth and you accepted it. Yet what he told you about Christmas was also the truth, yet you rejected it." If you would have seen the look on his face, he was really shaken. He asked me to give him the information on the books he needed to read that would confirm what I spoke on Christmas. I love this; he did not just accept what was spoken to him. He wanted the evidence. I gave him the scriptures and a list of historical books and he departed.

That night, when I returned to work, my friend met me and said he and his wife went to the Christian bookstore and found all the books on the list. They spent the day going through them and evaluating the information with the scriptures I gave them to support my point. He said, "Will, you were right; Christmas has nothing to do with God."

God is so good. He was right; just drop the seed and leave the rest up to Him. I was learning a lesson that when the truth is embedded in your heart, even if you initially reject it, God has a way of making it grow. Over the years I have seen this same scenario play out with people rejecting my teaching on Christmas just to come back later into agreement with it. Most of these saints did not even have half the information that I will be sharing with you in this book.

I have also been a teacher in bonds when it came to teaching the truth on the mark of the beast. Many times over the years, I have started teaching on the mark only to have God stop me. He would let me know it was not the time. The information on the mark, number, and the image of the beast is going to be riveting.

Over the years, I have seen so many theories and concepts on the mark of the best. All of them end with the same problem. They are trying to answer a dark saying (riddle) from the Bible using sources other than the Bible. I explained in my last book "Hidden in the Garden" that you cannot do this, when it comes to **metaphors** you have to allow the Bible to interpret itself.

I know many of you have heard over the years that the mark of the beast that goes on the right hand and forehead is a computer chip. As they start to place chips into people, many are seeing this as a confirmation of what they believe. There is deception behind this because the mark of the beast has been around for more than two thousand years. I will be showing this and exposing what the mark really is, according to what scripture teaches, not man's interpretation. The truth on the mark is going to be shocking and even more shocking will be how it is tied into Christmas. Gird up the loins of your mind and get ready, this is going to be an exciting yet edifying journey into Biblical understanding.

Sidenote: In my earlier books, I explain why I use the King James Version (KJV) of the Bible in most of my scripture quotes. Some readers have explained to me that they read my books with one of the modern versions of the Bible to compare with the King James Version and this makes it easier to understand. I still use the KJV because many of the modern versions have omitted or changed words to remove unpopular understandings of the scripture. Christ actually prophesied that this would happen (Matt 23:13). I also try to explain the scriptures so the reader will have a clear understanding. I do not believe King James is perfect because it has its problems also but the closer you can get to the original Hebrew and Greek manuscripts the less problems of interpretation you will face. Do not run away from the KJV strive to understand it because if you spend enough time in it the old English will read just like present day English in your mind.

Quotes from the book "A Dictionary of Early Christian Beliefs" are notated by DECB with the date noted by c (Common Era) as the date and numerical location of the quote in the writing.

Chapter 1

God is not Dead, He's Still Alive, He's Still Alive

I was lying in bed in a trailer, about a football field distance away from the perimeter fence of a maximum-security Florida prison. (Wow, the places God will take us to and takes us from.) I had just finished working the night shift and had slept through the morning and afternoon. It was time for me to get up. I had a prayer group that met that day. I would be teaching so I needed to be early, but I was tired so I laid there on the edge of sleep.

It came out of nowhere, which is commonplace when God speaks to you. I heard the voice say, "If Moses was dead, why did I speak to him out of the bush?" I had gotten accustomed to God speaking to me as much as anyone can. It was not an everyday occurrence by any means but it happened enough to where I started to notice a pattern. He often talked to me or gave me a vision when I was coming out of sleep, or drifting off into a sudden deep sleep. For those of you who do not know what a vision is, think about a video screen opening up in your head. God will use the screen to show you a video containing a message He wants you to know. Visions can take place when you are asleep or awake. He will also say things in a way that will make me think so that the message would be cemented into my mind. God would not say, "The sky is blue," because you would agree and then just drift back to sleep, only to awaken later and not even remember what was said because there was no process of thinking. He would instead ask something like, "Why isn't the sky red?" His statement would immediately make you think and the process of meditating on the question and formulating an answer would stamp the remembrance of the occurrence in your mind.

This question woke me up because it made no sense. I lifted my head off the pillow, wide-awake. When God asks me a question, I know there is a teaching point coming. He is trying to open up my understanding on something important. In addition, it makes me think. The question made no sense because Moses was not dead when God spoke to him through the ministering angel, the flame of fire on the bush.

Heb 1:7
7 And of the angels he saith, Who maketh his angels spirits, and **his ministers a flame of fire.**
KJV

Acts 7:30-31
30 And when forty years were expired, there appeared to him in the wilderness of mount Sina an angel of the Lord in a **flame of fire** in a bush.
31 When Moses saw it, he wondered at the sight: and as he drew near to behold it, **the voice of the Lord came unto him,**
KJV

So many times God has spoken to me in a short nonsensical statement, to the point that I am ready to rebuke it because I think it cannot be from God. Later, what He said would play out or He would give me the understanding and it would blow my mind. All I did here was reply that Moses wasn't dead and there was silence, nothing else was said.

I got up and got ready, feeling a little frustrated. It was almost Saturday, which was when I taught Bible study. I thought that the question had something to do with what He wanted me to teach. I had already prepared another lesson, of twenty pages or so, that had nothing to do with Moses and the burning bush. I got dressed, exited my home, entered my car, turned on the ignition, and the CD player started playing. These are the first words that came out of the speaker, **"My God is not dead, He's still alive, He's still alive!"**

There are no coincidences with God. I knew that more was coming and sure enough, the Holy Spirit started downloading.

As I started driving, I was asked (not audibly but in my spirit), "What does Abraham Lincoln, George Washington, and Martin Luther King have in common?" The conversation switched to something that is hard to explain to those who have never experienced it. In scripture it is called a "word of knowledge" where you are not told something, you just know it, with no explanation of how other than God. Instead of hearing, "The sky is blue," you just know it is blue, why it is blue, how it is blue, and how long it will be blue. It is an instantaneous download of information.

I responded that those three men were all leaders and they are all dead. They did great things, and therefore we celebrate their birthdays in memory of them. This is normal. All over the world, we remember our great men and women who have passed on by giving them a national holiday and celebrating their birthdays. Makes sense!

Then the question came, "If I am not dead, then why are they celebrating My birthday?" It made sense now. The same way that God was not speaking to a dead man (Moses), He wants us to know and show in our actions that we are not speaking to a dead Savior! (Christ is the part of the Father sent to reveal all of the Father to men. He is God in the flesh.) **We have national holidays for dead men on their birthdays. Neither the Father nor Christ is dead.**

Christ promise in scripture that if we love Him and keep His commandments, then He and the Father will love us and manifest in our lives. This is the norm. God talks to and fellowships with all His children, this is a fundamental truth. If you are His, He will communicate with you. Yet today, we have pastors that have never heard a word from God and do not realize that something is wrong. God promises that if you draw close to Him, He will draw close to you. God keeps His promises.

John 14:21
21 He that hath my commandments, and keepeth them, he it is that loveth me: and he that loveth me shall be loved of my Father, and I will love him, and **will manifest myself to him.**

It's Your Birthday

I want you to picture yourself opening up your front door and entering your home. It is dark, so you reach over and turn on the light and get startled by a house full of people screaming, "Surprise, happy birthday!" You then say to your friends, "But it is not my birthday." You stare and wonder why everyone is celebrating your birthday on the wrong day and why none of them took the time to ask you for the correct day.

Christ was not born on December 25, no way and no how. If we say that we are in a relationship with Him and He speaks to us, then why is it that He has not given the correct date to someone? I asked Him but before I reveal what He told me, let me share with you proof that it could not be December 25.

I have noticed that God gives many warnings in scripture concerning how we worship Him. Over and over again, He has warned that man does not decide how to worship God and all worship should be according to what He has given in scripture. **Even the Son points out that if we are worshiping according to the commandments of men, then this worship is in vain. I want to reiterate this; any worship of the Son that comes from the commandments of men is in vain. It is worthless.**

Mark 7:7
7 Howbeit in vain do they worship me, teaching for doctrines **the commandments of men.**
KJV

When God spoke to Israel, as they entered the Promised Land, He gave them a strong warning against observing how other nations worshipped their gods and then utilizing these methods to worship Him. He pointed out that much of what is done as worship among the nations are an abomination to Him, and they were forbidden from worshipping Him in like manner.

Deut 12:28-32
28 Observe and hear all these words which I command thee, that it may go well with thee, and with thy children after thee for ever, when

thou doest that which is good and right in the sight of the LORD thy God.

29 When the LORD thy God shall cut off the nations from before thee, whither thou goest to possess them, and thou succeedest them, and dwellest in their land;

30 **Take heed to thyself that thou be not snared by following them**, after that they be destroyed from before thee; and that thou inquire not after their gods, saying, How did these nations serve their gods? even so will I do likewise.

31 **Thou shalt not do so unto the LORD thy God: for every abomination to the LORD, which he hateth, have they done unto their gods**; for even their sons and their daughters they have burnt in the fire to their gods.

32 **What thing soever I command you, observe to do it: thou shalt not add thereto, nor diminish from it.**
KJV

Do not let anyone fool you; the celebration of Christ is worship. Everything we do in the worship of God has to be according to what He teaches, not what we come up with. So my question to you is, "Where in scripture does God command or even suggest an annual celebration to be held to glorify Christ's birthday on December 25"? Where? After the initial proclamation of Christ's birth, we find nowhere else in scripture anyone celebrating His birthday. You have to understand that the books of the New Testament span approximately 100 years after Christ entered the world as the child that was to be the Lamb of God. Nowhere in scripture, after Mary gave birth, do you hear anything about the celebration of the birth of Christ. The average believer is not aware of this, and they don't realize that the early church fathers ridiculed the pagans for celebrating the birthday of their false gods.

WHERE IN THE BIBLE ARE WE INSTRUCTED TO HAVE AN ANNUAL CELEBRATION OF CHRIST'S BIRTHDAY?

Arnobius, one of the early church fathers during the time when there was no annual celebration of Christ's birth, contrasted between the early church and the pagan celebrations surrounding them.

<u>Humans have birthdays, so the pagans believe that the powers of heaven have birthdays, too.</u> *Arnobius* (ce. 305, E), 6.532 DECB pg 342

The truth of the matter is that it took 300 years before the Church started celebrating Christ's birthday and this was sanctioned by the Roman Church that was already deeply involved in pagan worship. The Roman church also gave the date of December 25, which coincided with the birthday of many pagan gods. Men added this worship; it was not ordained by God. We have already answered the question, "Does the Father or Christ accept worship ordained by men?"

Matt 15:8-9
8 This people draweth nigh unto me with their mouth, and honoureth me with their lips; but their heart is far from me.
9 **But in vain they do worship me, teaching for doctrines the commandments of men**.
KJV

Proverbs with its wisdom points out that when we add to the Word of God we will be exposed as liars.

Prov 30:6
6 Add thou not unto his words, lest he reprove thee, and thou be found a liar.
KJV

December 25th, no way no how

Let's first expose the lie about the date. We have clues in scripture that point to why it could not be wintertime when Christ was born. The first is the reason why Jesus' parents, Joseph and Mary, were in Bethlehem.

Luke 2:1-7
2:1 And it came to pass in those days, that **there went out a decree from Caesar Augustus, that all the world should be taxed.**
2(And this taxing was first made when Cyrenius was governor of Syria.)

3 And **all went to be taxed, every one into his own city.**
4 And Joseph also went up from Galilee, out of the city of Nazareth, into Judaea, unto the city of David, which is called Bethlehem; (because he was of the house and lineage of David:)
5 **To be taxed with Mary his espoused wife, being great with child.**
6 And so it was, that, while they were there, the days were accomplished that she should be delivered.
7 And she brought forth her firstborn son, and wrapped him in swaddling clothes, and laid him in a manger; because there was no room for them in the inn.
KJV

If you do a study of Roman history, you will realize that when a census tax was taken it was not done in the winter. As we can see by the scriptures, all those who were to be counted and taxed, had to return to their place of birth. There would be a lot of traveling, and the winter would not be the time you would want all this movement taking place. For us to understand the harshness of winter in Judea during Christ's time, all we have to do is read Christ's remarks that the people pray that they don't have to flee for their lives in winter.

Mark 13:17-18
17 But woe to them that are with child, and to them that give suck in those days!
18 And **pray ye that your flight be not in the winter.**
KJV

Christ warns of the harshness of winter, much less to have a woman nine months pregnant (Mary) traveling at that time.

Another point to be noted is that taxes were held around the time of harvest because this is the time when the people had the most money after selling their crops. Harvest is never in wintertime, so this again supports the fact that Christ was not born on December 25.

The third point that many miss is that the angel made the proclamation of Christ's birth to the shepherds who had their flocks out in the night and this could not be in the dead of winter.

Luke 2:8-11
8 And there were in the same country **shepherds abiding in the field, keeping watch over their flock by night.**
9 And, lo, the angel of the Lord came upon them, and the glory of the Lord shone round about them: and they were sore afraid.
10 And the angel said unto them, Fear not: for, behold, I bring you good tidings of great joy, which shall be to all people.
11 For unto you is born this day in the city of David a Saviour, which is Christ the Lord.
KJV

It is obvious when you look at the scriptures that it is not possible for December 25 to be the day when Jesus was born.

1. Taxes were taken around the time of a harvest! There is no harvest in December.
2. Mary was "great with child." She would not have been traveling in the dead of winter, especially if Christ stated it is harsh to flee for your life in winter.
3. Shepherds also would not have their flocks out at that time.

Most Christian leaders today will tell you that they are aware that December 25th is not when Jesus was born. So why was the 25th of December chosen as the date? I can picture someone holding up a calendar and throwing a dart; wherever it lands that will be the date. Truth be told many Christian leaders who study history know why they chose that date but they will not tell it. (More Later.)

Many years ago, I was preparing a lesson to teach on Christmas (soon after God had released me to teach on the subject). I prayed and asked God to guide me in the preparation of the lesson. I wanted His confirmation because I wanted to make sure I was not operating on my own devices. This is what Christ spoke to me:

"If man is hearing from the Holy Spirit, which is the Spirit of Truth, and God wanted them to celebrate Christ's birthday, **don't you think I would reveal the true date? I have no Birthday!**
A son is given!
A child is born!"

When this was spoken into my spirit, my first understanding was it is obvious that if we are to celebrate (which is to worship) the birthday of Christ, God would have given somebody the correct date. Scripture confirms this fact.

I want you to understand this clearly. Jesus was speaking to a Samaritan woman by a well (John 4). The Samaritans were a mixture of people brought into the land of Israel from different conquered nations by the Assyrians and Babylonians. They mixed with the Israelites that were left in the land when God exiled the people to Babylon. These people syncretized (mixed) their pagan beliefs with the worship of Yahweh, and the Jews saw them as an abomination and would not even sit to eat with them. Their way of worship was not the truth of what God gave to Israel.

When Christ was at a well, a woman asked Him why as a Jew did he ask her for water when Jews would have nothing to do with her people? Christ took the opportunity to instruct her on salvation. The woman proclaimed that her people worshiped God in the mountain where the well was located. Christ then proclaims to her a powerful truth that shines a light on what is so wrong with Christmas:

John 4:21-24
21 Jesus saith unto her, Woman, believe me, the hour cometh, when ye shall neither in this mountain, nor yet at Jerusalem, worship the Father.
22 Ye worship ye know not what: we know what we worship: for salvation is of the Jews.
23 But the hour cometh, and now is, when the true worshippers shall worship the Father in spirit and in truth: for the Father seeketh such to worship him.
24 **God is a Spirit: and they that worship him must worship him in spirit and in truth.**
KJV

This is not just an apostle or prophet speaking, this is Christ the Lamb of God. He points out to the woman that her people really do not understand what they are worshiping. The Samarians had incorporated their traditions from the worship of other gods into their failed attempt to worship Yahweh (this is why the Jews rejected them). **When you combine rituals from the worship of other gods and try to utilize them in the worship of the one and only true God, you are worshiping in error.** Christ points out that the Jews know what they worship. What Christ is saying is that God has instructed the Jews (Israel) in the proper way of worship.

Christ goes on to show the woman that a change is coming, and God is revealing that true spiritual worship will not be on the mountain or in Jerusalem. He is showing that the worship done in the mountain is corrupt and even in Jerusalem it has become corrupted and now God, the Creator of the universe, is seeking a people that will worship Him in spirit and in truth. I must reiterate this point. He is emphasizing that now is the time when **all** worshipers of God must do it in spirit and in truth. God is seeking individuals who are willing to say that all worship of God must be in spirit and in truth and then walk in what they confess.

Does Christmas stand up to this litmus test? No, Christmas does not, and I can prove it. The celebration of Christmas is full of many lies that the average believer is unaware of, but we will be shining a light on them later in this book. Before we get to that let's look more closely at the last part of what I was told.

I have no birthday!
A son is given!
A child is born!

I know many people will say that we are celebrating when He came into the world, but you might want to check your Bible. **Christ did not enter the world when Mary gave birth to Jesus.** Who do you think was in the garden? Who do you think talked with Abraham? (Christ said, "Before Abraham was, I Am.")

John 8:58
58 Jesus said unto them, Verily, verily, I say unto you, **Before Abraham was, I am.**
KJV

If no one has ever seen the Father as scripture testifies, then who were they looking upon in the Old Testament?

John 6:46

46 **Not that any man hath seen the Father**, save he which is of God, he hath seen the Father.

Christ was a Son long before He came as a child. The Son that was given was born of God long before He came as a man. He always existed, no beginning and no ending. He has no birthday.

Heb 7:3

3 **Without father, without mother, without descent, having neither beginning of days, nor end of life; but made like unto the Son of God**; abideth a priest continually.
KJV

Christ has no beginning of days and He has no ending of life. He did not leave any instruction on the celebration of His birthday because He has none. This is what the early church father Arnobius understood. His time in the earth as the Lamb of God made it necessary that He put on the flesh of a man. Every day that we walk in His will, we celebrate His life, death, and resurrection in the flesh that provided our redemption. The reason none of the believers in the New Testament had an annual celebration for His birth goes beyond him not leaving instructions. The early believers understood the powerful revelation in a verse left to us by Paul.

I want you to close your eyes and picture Christ in your mind. I guarantee that ninety-nine percent of the people reading this book pictured Him as an image that is not who He is today. You pictured Christ in the flesh as a child, man, or on the cross. Why is it that so many see Him in the flesh? Why is it when we walk into the majority of Christian churches, we see Christ on the cross or as He walked in the flesh? Is this the last picture of Christ left to us in the Bible? Do you realize that the image that John saw in Revelation is the image of Christ today? Do you realize it is the image of the Father the Ancient of Days? (See Daniel 7:9-10)

2 Cor 5:16
16 Wherefore henceforth know we no man after the flesh: yea, **though we have known Christ after the flesh, yet now henceforth know we him no more.**
KJV

Paul is saying that when we see one another, do not see or have an understanding based upon the flesh you see before you. See the person as a new creation of God, a spiritual child of God. In the same way, He says we should no longer see Christ as a child, man, or even as the Lamb of God. We are to see Christ as what He was before He came as the Lamb of God and that is the same image that He is today. Even Christ points to this when He asked the Father to give Him back the glory that He had before the world was:

John 17:5
5 And now, O Father, glorify thou me with **thine own self** with **the glory which I had with thee before the world was.**
KJV

Christ put back on the glory of God's own self; He became what He was from before eternity.

Matt 28:18-20
18 And Jesus came and spake unto them, saying, **All power is given unto me in heaven and in earth.**
19 Go ye therefore, and teach all nations, baptizing them in the name of the Father, and of the Son, and of the Holy Ghost:
20 **Teaching them to observe all things whatsoever I have commanded you**: and, lo, I am with you alway, even unto the end of the world. Amen.
KJV

Ask yourself this question, "Did Christ leave us a command to celebrate Christmas?" No, He did not, and that is why none of the Apostles taught us to observe it. This is in accordance with what He commanded in verse 20.

When we picture Christ, we are to picture Him with all power in heaven and on earth. We are to see Jesus as He is and not only what He was. Let's look at the prophecy where God says a child is born and a son is given. Read carefully and ask yourself, which Christ is being described? Is it the suffering servant or the all-powerful Son of God?

Isa 9:6-7
6 For unto us a child is born, unto us a son is given: and **the government shall be upon his shoulder:** and his name shall be called **Wonderful, Counsellor, The mighty God, The everlasting Father, The Prince of Peace.**
7 Of the increase of his government and peace there shall be no end, upon the throne of David, and upon his kingdom, to order it, and to establish it with judgment and with justice from henceforth even for ever. The zeal of the LORD of hosts will perform this.
KJV

When we picture Christ as a babe in the manger or a dying man on the cross, we see the limitations of the man He became to die for our sins. Paul understands that we limit Christ when all we can see is who He was in the flesh. When we see Him as described in Rev 1:12-18 with all power, then we see the power flowing through the Church His Body because we are seeing the truth of who He is. When we can see Christ as He truly is today, then we can realize that we as His body have the power of God flowing through us. We can see who we really are when we are walking in the Spirit, which is abiding in Christ. We are new creatures who have access to the Armor of God with the Power of God flowing through us. Realizing and visualizing who Christ really is, reveals who we really are in Him. If we can see the truth of who He is, then we can see the truth of who we are in Him. When we walk in this truth, then demons tremble before us. This wisdom is a weapon against the lies of the enemy who does not want us to realize what we have in Christ. This is the Christ we serve:

Rev 1:12-18
12 And I turned to see the voice that spake with me. And being turned, I saw seven golden candlesticks;
13 And in the midst of the seven candlesticks one like unto the Son of man, clothed with a garment down to the foot, and girt about the paps with a golden girdle.

14 His head and his hairs were white like wool, as white as snow; and his eyes were as a flame of fire;
15 And his feet like unto fine brass, as if they burned in a furnace; and his voice as the sound of many waters.
16 And he had in his right hand seven stars: and out of his mouth went a sharp twoedged sword: and his countenance was as the sun shineth in his strength.
17 And when I saw him, I fell at his feet as dead. And he laid his right hand upon me, saying unto me, Fear not; I am the first and the last:
18 I am he that liveth, and was dead; and, behold, I am alive for evermore, Amen; and have the keys of hell and of death.
KJV

He left a commandment to go and teach all nations to observe **all He commanded**. Again, did Christ command anyone to celebrate or observe Christmas? He didn't. The Christ who is our Master is not a child in a manger or the Lamb of God on the cross. Those are what He became, not what He is. We acknowledge and embrace the birth and the death, but the resurrected glorified Christ is the Head of the Body. He is all-powerful. He left one commandment of what we should do to remember His life, death, and resurrection, which we will discuss at the end of the book.

The devil wants us to only see Christ as He was in the flesh because he knows that subconsciously it limits our understanding of who Christ really is and who we are in Him. Now that we understand this, let's look at what Paul said one more time:

2 Cor 5:16-17
16 Wherefore we henceforth know no man after the flesh: even though we have known Christ after the flesh, yet now we know (him so) no more.
17 **Wherefore if any man is in Christ, (he is) a new creature: the old things are passed away; behold, they are become new.**
ASV

I want you to read this carefully: **When we can see who Christ really is, then we can see who we really are in Him, and then we can become who God truly intended us to be.** God intended us to be spiritual minded sons of God. Through the Spirit, we are able to overcome the flesh. When we walk in the spiritual understanding, which is walking in the Spirit, we can overcome the flesh.

Rom 8:1-14
8:1 Free from Indwelling Sin
There is therefore now no condemnation to those who are in Christ Jesus, who do not walk according to the flesh, but according to the Spirit. 2 For the law of the Spirit of life in Christ Jesus has made me free from the law of sin and death. 3 For what the law could not do in that it was weak through the flesh, God did by sending His own Son in the likeness of sinful flesh, on account of sin: He condemned sin in the flesh, 4 that the righteous requirement of the law might be fulfilled in us who do not walk according to the flesh but according to the Spirit. 5 For those who live according to the flesh set their minds on the things of the flesh, but those who live according to the Spirit, the things of the Spirit. 6 For to be carnally minded is death, but to be spiritually minded is life and peace. 7 Because the carnal mind is enmity against God; for it is not subject to the law of God, nor indeed can be. 8 So then, those who are in the flesh cannot please God. 9 But you are not in the flesh but in the Spirit, if indeed the Spirit of God dwells in you. Now if anyone does not have the Spirit of Christ, he is not His. 10 And if Christ is in you, the body is dead because of sin, but the Spirit is life because of righteousness. 11 But if the Spirit of Him who raised Jesus from the dead dwells in you, He who raised Christ from the dead will also give life to your mortal bodies through His Spirit who dwells in you.

12 Sonship Through the Spirit
Therefore, brethren, we are debtors — not to the flesh, to live according to the flesh. 13 For **if you live according to the flesh you will die**; but **if by the Spirit you put to death the deeds of the body, you will live.** 14 For as many as are led by the Spirit of God, these are sons of God.
NKJV

Do you realize that understanding who Christ is spiritually is the key to overcoming the flesh because it reveals who we are spiritually? Paul was teaching the believer to let go of who Christ was in the flesh and see Him, as He truly is, which reveals who we really are. Therefore, my question is, "Does Christmas celebrate Christ in the spirit or in the flesh?" Where is the celebration of the all-powerful Messiah glorified with the Father's own self? Why do we not celebrate Christ as He is today?

The world won't accept the true Christ

Why is it that the world won't accept anything of God **yet almost every nation and every people accepts Christmas?** We know the world is carnal, and Christians are supposed to be spiritual. Look at all the celebrations of Christmas and tell me how much is carnal and how much is spiritual. I have found over the years that nothing I have taught brings as much condemnation from the world as my teachings of the truth about Christmas. Some don't even believe in God but they will beat you down if you talk against their Christmas. Why is this?

Gal 4:29
29 But as then he that was born after the flesh persecuted him that was born after the Spirit, even so it is now.

All the world is doing is glorifying the flesh that Christ came in! If you take a close examination of what is done by the world in celebrating Christmas, you will see it is obvious. The shameful part is that some of the same things we use to celebrate Christ originated from the worship of pagan gods. These gods are identified by God as devils and demons. Why would God accept this?

Three wise men

I want to address another misconception that reveals the celebration of Christmas is operating in everything but the truth. All over the world, you will see nativity scenes set up with the three wise men handing gifts to Joseph and Mary for the newborn Christ sitting in a basket in the manger. This is one of the biggest falsehoods tied into Christmas.

The wise men were **never** at Jesus' birth and there was no mention of **three** wise men in the Bible. Let's take a closer look at the scriptural evidence.

Matt 2:1-8
2:1 Now when Jesus was born in Bethlehem of Judaea in the days of Herod the king, behold, there came **wise men** from the east to Jerusalem,
2 Saying, Where is he that is born King of the Jews? **for we have seen his star in the east,** and are come to worship him.
3 When Herod the king had heard these things, he was troubled, and all Jerusalem with him.
4 And when he had gathered all the chief priests and scribes of the people together, he demanded of them where Christ should be born.
5 And they said unto him, In Bethlehem of Judaea: for thus it is written by the prophet,
6 And thou Bethlehem, in the land of Juda, art not the least among the princes of Juda: for out of thee shall come a Governor, that shall rule my people Israel.
7 Then Herod, when he had privily called **the wise men**, inquired of them diligently **what time the star appeared.**
8 And he sent them to Bethlehem, and said, Go and search diligently for the young child; and when ye have found him, bring me word again, that I may come and worship him also.
KJV

I want you to notice that nowhere in the story is the number **three** ever mentioned as you often hear in the traditions attributed to Christmas. You cannot mix an untruth into the worship of God. When Christ says, "In spirit and in truth," He means it.

I want you to picture a group (not three) of wise men somewhere in the east (tradition sites Babylonia region) watching the skies one night and then they see a star appear that they realize signifies the birth of the King of the Jews. The wise men then gather themselves together, drive down to the local airport, and fly to Jerusalem to ask where the King of the Jews is and the scribes in Jerusalem point out He is to be born in Bethlehem. The wise men then call the local Uber, jump into the cars, and rush over to Bethlehem in time to see Jesus lying in a manger. Oh, wait a minute, this happened two thousand years ago. There were no planes, uber, or vehicles. Are you starting to get the picture?

Now, let's look at what would have really happened. Wise men in the Far East are watching the skies and they see a star appear that signifies that the King of the Jews has been born in Judea. In the morning, they send out word to other wise men and gather to discuss what they should do. They decide that they will prepare a caravan to journey to Judea to honor the newborn king. Days if not weeks of preparation goes into gathering goods, animals, and other supplies that will be needed for the trip. We have to realize that these groups of men could be traveling hundreds if not thousands of miles to get to Judea. Unlike today, the travel in ancient times could be perilous and the preparation period could be longer than the travel time itself.

After the preparation, the group would set out to travel to Judea. Many places they would be traveling through were areas where there were no roads. The journey consisted of crossing rivers, going over mountains, and entering foreign territories.

The truth of the matter is that this journey at the least would have been weeks and could take as long as years to complete. We do not need to wonder because scripture points to a reasonable understanding of how long it took them to get to Bethlehem. Take note of the words in bold in the rest of the story from the scriptures below:

Matt 2:3-12
3 When Herod the king had heard these things, he was troubled, and all Jerusalem with him.
4 And when he had gathered all the chief priests and scribes of the people together, he demanded of them where Christ should be born.
5 And they said unto him, In Bethlehem of Judaea: for thus it is written by the prophet,
6 And thou Bethlehem, in the land of Juda, art not the least among the princes of Juda: for out of thee shall come a Governor, that shall rule my people Israel.
7 **Then Herod, when he had privily called the wise men, inquired of them diligently what time the star appeared.**

8 And he sent them to Bethlehem, and said, Go and **search diligently for the young child**; and when ye have found him, bring me word again, that I may come and worship him also.

9 When they had heard the king, they departed; and, lo, the star, which they saw in the east, went before them, till it came and stood over where the young child was.

10 When they saw the star, they rejoiced with exceeding great joy.

11 And when they were come into **the house**, they saw **the young child** with Mary his mother, and fell down, and worshipped him: and when they had opened their treasures, they presented unto him gifts; gold, and frankincense, and myrrh.

12 And being warned of God in a dream that they should not return to Herod, they departed into their **own country** another way.

KJV

In verse 7, we see that Herod wanted to know exactly what time the star appeared. Herod already knew that he was going to kill the child, because as king of Judea the child Jesus, in his eyes, threatened his own rule over the region. He needed to know exactly when the star was seen so he could calculate the age of the child. Knowing the age would allow him to identify the child. This is the key to understanding how long it took the wise men to get to Judea. Also, notice the wise men entered into a house and not a manger (stable). The nativity scene that we are used to seeing is proven inaccurate because the wise men were neither at Christ's birth nor ever in the manger. Truth be told, it was close to two years before they got to Judea and scripture reveals this to those paying attention.

Please read this carefully:

Matt 2:16

16 Then Herod, when he saw that he was mocked of the wise men, was exceeding wroth, and sent forth, and slew all the children that were in Bethlehem, and in all the coasts thereof, **from two years old and under, according to the time which he had diligently inquired of the wise men.**

KJV

The scripture reveals that Christ was about two years old when the wise men got to Bethlehem to honor the young Savior.

Scripture will always reveal the truth that unravels the lies of tradition.

Jesus was not born in the winter, there is no indication of **"three"** wise men, they were not at His birth, they were never in the manger, and He was around two years old before they even laid eyes on Him. God is still seeking the true worshipers who are willing to cast off the lies and worship Him in Spirit and in truth. Are you ready to go deeper into the truth about Christmas? I promise you that this journey will be well worth it, for those heaven-bent on making it into the Kingdom, but it will be painful because it is necessary to uproot false beliefs tied into the tradition of men. Take a deep breath we are going deeper.

Chapter 2

Pressure and Persecution

I want you to understand that there is no record of a single apostle celebrating Christ's Birthday. There is not a single line of historical confirmation of any disciple, who lived during the time of Christ, ever celebrating His birthday. There is no record of a single person taught by the apostles having ever celebrated the birthday of Christ. There is not one single iota of evidence that those who were taught by those taught by the apostles, having ever celebrated His birthday. The average believer today that is truly trying to serve God is not aware of this and this allows the enemy to pull the wool over their eyes.

It normally takes three or four generations before a group loses the remembrance of what was left to them from the first generation. Understand it like this: Most of us have memories of our grandparents but few if any remember our great-grandparents. If you are going to implement something that goes against the teachings of the first generation, it will be more effective to wait until after the third or fourth generation. This would ensure that all who were taught by the first generation were gone. The last apostle to die was John, who died in Ephesus around 100 ce. Three generations (70 years per generation) later would put us at around 310 ce.

According to a Roman almanac, the Christian festival of Christmas was celebrated in Rome by ad 336. Note the name Christmas (Christ-Mass). Mass is a term used in the Roman Catholic Church, not the Bible.

Sidenote: This is long after the death of the last disciple and right before the Roman church (now the Roman Catholic church) took complete authority over all Churches in the western hemisphere (stating to the people That God had given all authority on earth to the Pope).

I want to give you a short history lesson of what was taking place from the time of Christ's death and resurrection to the time Rome became the strongest force in the Christian movement. After Christ's death and resurrection, the majority of the persecution against Christians came from the Jews. The Christian church was growing immensely, especially during the first three and a half years after the crucifixion.

Christ instructed the apostles to go to the lost sheep of Israel only. Very few people realize that the Jewish people had three and a half years after the resurrection to accept the Messiah. This is what Daniel wrote about in his book.

Dan 9:24-27

24 **Seventy weeks** are determined upon thy people and upon thy holy city, to finish the transgression, and to make an end of sins, and to make reconciliation for iniquity, and to bring in everlasting righteousness, and to seal up the vision and prophecy, and **to anoint the most Holy.**

25 Know therefore and understand, that from the going forth of the commandment to restore and to build Jerusalem unto the Messiah the Prince shall be seven weeks, and threescore and two weeks: the street shall be built again, and the wall, even in troublous times.

26 And **after threescore and two weeks shall Messiah be cut off, but not for himself:** and the people of the prince that shall come shall destroy the city and the sanctuary; and the end thereof shall be with a flood, and unto the end of the war desolations are determined.

27 And **he shall confirm the covenant with many for one week: and in the midst of the week he shall cause the sacrifice and the oblation to cease,** and for the overspreading of abominations he shall make it desolate, even until the consummation, and that determined shall be poured upon the desolate.

KJV

The angel Gabriel is giving Daniel a correct interpretation of the dark saying prophecy. He tells him that God has determined seventy weeks for the people of Israel. Remember, the Julian calendar did not exist at this time. There was no such thing as the word "week". The word, translated week, is "shabuwa," which means seven. The seventy weeks is actually seventy times seven years because the week is seven years not days. Example:

Gen 29:27
27 Fulfil her **week**, and we will give thee this also for the service which thou shalt serve with me **yet seven other years**.
KJV

Week equals seven years in this verse just like in Daniel. Gabriel says seventy sevens (weeks). Therefore, he is saying that Daniel's people have 70 times 7 years, which equals 490 years that have been determined for his people. They have 490 years to end sin, to be forgiven for their sin, to receive eternal righteousness, to fulfill all visions and prophecy, and anoint the Messiah (most Holy). Simplified, Israel has 490 years to get their act together to receive the Messiah. Gabriel then gives Daniel the starting point for the years. He also tells him what will take place before the Messiah comes. He says 49 years (seven weeks of seven years) and 434 years (threescore and two weeks of seven years). I believe the 49 years was the time it took for them to rebuild the city. From the end of the rebuilding period until messiah shows up would then be 434 years. That is a total of 483 years of the 490. When Messiah showed up there would be seven years left. Christ entered Jerusalem to start a seven-year ministry that is the last week or last seven years of the prophecy. Gabriel goes on to say that, the Messiah would be killed after 62 weeks or 434 year period (plus the 49 year rebuilding gives us a total of 483 years).

Dan 9:26
26 And **after** threescore and two weeks shall **Messiah be cut off,** but not for himself: and the people of **the prince that shall come shall destroy the city and the sanctuary; and the end thereof shall be with a flood, and unto the end of the war desolations are determined.**
KJV

Gabriel goes on to say that after the Messiah is killed (cut off) that a prince shall come and destroy the city. This is exactly what happened in 70 ce when the Roman army destroyed Jerusalem. Gabriel then goes back and gives further details of what is going to happen:

Dan 9:27
27 And **he shall confirm the covenant with many for one week**: and **in the midst of the week** he shall cause the sacrifice and the oblation to cease, and for the overspreading of abominations he shall make it desolate, even until the consummation, and that determined shall be poured upon the desolate.
KJV

This is where many make a mistake interpreting the prophecy because the details come after. He will make a covenant and in the middle of the week (three and a half of the seven years) stops the sin sacrifices. They believe the one making the covenant is the prince that is going to destroy the city, but it is not. Christ is crucified in the middle of His seven years ministry and that ends the acceptance by God of all sacrifices from the temple. Christ was killed after three and a half years of His ministry (the midpoint of the last week). Christ became the last sacrifice because after He died as the Lamb of God, there would be no more sacrifice for sin. Remember, His ministry was for seven years so even after His death His ministry to the Jews continued. This is why Christ told the apostles to go to the lost sheep of Israel only. The last three and a half years of His ministry to the Jews had to be completed.

Matt 15:23-24
23 But he answered her not a word. And his disciples came and besought him, saying, Send her away; for she crieth after us.
24 But he answered and said, **I am not sent but unto the lost sheep of the house of Israel.**
KJV

Matt 10:5-6
5 These twelve Jesus sent forth, and commanded them, saying, **Go not into the way of the Gentiles, and into any city of the Samaritans enter ye not:**
6 But go rather **to the lost sheep of the house of Israel.** KJV

Christ was not lying. He was first sent to the lost house of Israel during His ministry here on earth. The Father knew what the Jews were going to do, yet they were still allotted seven years according to Daniel's prophecy. During the first few years, the building up of the church was through a majority of Jewish followers, and the persecution came mostly from the Jewish establishment. After the seven years were completed and the nation, in general had rejected the Messiah, as foretold in prophecy, salvation was extended to the Gentiles. Apostle Peter was told to go to Cornelius (a Gentile), and Paul was struck down on Damascus road in preparation for his calling to salvation so he also could be sent to the Gentiles. Christ actually spoke of this happening in His parable of the wedding. Those bidden to the wedding were the Jews invited to salvation:

Matt 22:4-10
4 Again, he sent forth other servants, saying, **Tell them which are bidden,** Behold, I have prepared my dinner: my oxen and my fatlings are killed, and all things are ready: come unto the marriage.
5 But they made light of it, and went their ways, one to his farm, another to his merchandise:
6 And the remnant took his servants, and entreated them spitefully, and slew them.
7 But when the king heard thereof, he was wroth: and he sent forth his armies, and **destroyed those murderers, and burned up their city.**
8 Then saith he to his servants, The wedding is ready, but they which were bidden were not worthy.
9 Go ye therefore into the highways, and as many as ye shall find, bid to the marriage.
10 So those servants went out into the highways, and gathered together all as many as they found, both bad and good: and the wedding was furnished with guests.
KJV

The king is God and His Son is Christ whose wedding the Jews were invited to, but they rejected the invitation and slew those who were sent to invite them. God then gives the command to burn up their city Jerusalem (destruction of the city took place in 70 ce) and extends the invitation to all that will accept. After the Jewish nation rejected Christ and murdered many apostles and followers of

Christ, the Romans came and just as Christ had foretold, Jerusalem was destroyed. The temple was burned down to the ground as Christ prophesied. Salvation then spread like wildfire among the Gentile nations but this did not stop the persecution, if anything it just increased it.

Loss of Revenue

One of the biggest "problems" with the spread of Christianity to the Gentiles was that with the number of people being converted, there were significantly fewer followers of the pagan gods. Christianity was spreading so fast that pagan temples were losing many of their followers. Understand that the temples were the cultural and financial epicenters of many of these city-states. These places of worship were used to maintain control of the masses. Those involved with the temples also used them to acquire wealth. This point is even confirmed in the New Testament scriptures:

Acts 19:24-28
24 For a certain man named Demetrius, a silversmith, which made silver shrines for Diana, **brought no small gain unto the craftsmen**;
25 Whom he called together with the workmen of like occupation, and said, Sirs, **ye know that by this craft we have our wealth.**
26 Moreover ye see and hear, that not alone at Ephesus, but almost throughout all Asia, this Paul hath persuaded and **turned away much people**, saying that they be no gods, which are made with hands:
27 So that not only this our craft is in danger to be set at nought; but also that the temple of the great goddess Diana should be despised, and her magnificence should be destroyed, whom all Asia and the world worshippeth.
28 And when they heard these sayings, they were full of wrath, and cried out, saying, Great is Diana of the Ephesians.
KJV

The church growth was hindering the financial control of those in power and this became a threat to many. The persecution of the church started anew as the leaders of the Gentiles saw Christianity as a threat.

Before we go further, I want you to think about something. **If someone today had solid proof that Christmas was not of God and the proof was so compelling that it threatened Christmas itself, what would be the reaction of those who are enriched by this holiday? Do you realize that Christmas is not a billion dollar business but a trillion dollar business?** Most stores make more money during the Christmas holiday season than the rest of the year. When you start messing with people's money, expect a lot of opposition, not to exclude the spiritual attacks that will come because the enemy understands full well what Christmas is really about. This is why those who are exposed to the truth are so shocked by the opposition they face when they start to share the knowledge. You will get a fight from family members, friends, and those you don't even know. You will sometimes feel like you have been ostracized; even your family will be against you. My question to you is, "Didn't Christ say this would happen when we confess the truth?" Be prepared also for the strong spiritual fight that will come. The whole world will be against you if you touch their Christmas. You are going to need to armor up. (Please read "The Armor of God (A Deeper understanding)" to learn how to armor up.)

As Christianity grew in numbers, there was an explosion of persecution against the Christian church. The Roman Empire was the leading force in many of the areas where Christianity was growing the fastest. North Africa, Asia, and Southern Europe were controlled by Rome. The Romans, shortly after the destruction of Jerusalem, renewed the persecution of the church. It seemed as if every problem that came up in the empire became the fault of the Christians. Christians were not people who were looking for rebellion like the Jews who wanted desperately to be freed from the Roman's control. Christians were the common people who were taught by the gospel to submit to those in authority and show kindness, even to their enemies. Yet they were hated beyond measure because their lifestyle brought conviction to others, and they became the scapegoats for every problem. If you want a more in-depth historical retelling of the events of the persecution, please take the time to read "Eusebius The Church Histories (Paul L. Maier)."

They persecute us, not from the supposition that we are wrong-doers, but imagining that by the very fact of our being Christians we sin against life. This is because of the way we conduct ourselves, and because we exhort theirs to adopt a similar life. *Clement of Alexandria* (c. 195,E), 2.423. DECB pg 509*

2 Tim 3:12-14
12 Yea, and all that will live godly in Christ Jesus shall suffer persecution.
13 But evil men and seducers shall wax worse and worse, deceiving, and being deceived.
14 But **continue thou in the things which thou hast learned and hast been assured of, knowing of whom thou hast learned them;**

     The message that the apostles left for the believers, was that we must expect persecution if we intend to live holy lives, as required by scriptures. The evil of humankind would only get worse. Yet they implored us to hold on to the teachings that we received from them assuring us that they were the teachings of Christ. They knew Christ and were anointed and placed in the ministry by Him so we could be assured of their teachings. **Any teaching, doctrine, tradition, or ritual that does not line up with what we were left by Christ, and the apostles needs to be rejected.**

Gal 1:6-12
6 I marvel that ye are so soon removed from him that called you into the grace of Christ unto another gospel:
7 Which is not another; but there be some that trouble you, and would pervert the gospel of Christ.
8 But **though we, or an angel from heaven, preach any other gospel unto you than that which we have preached unto you, let him be accursed.**
9 As we said before, so say I now again, If any man preach any other gospel unto you than that ye have received, let him be accursed .
10 For do I now persuade men, or God? or do I seek to please men? for if I yet pleased men, I should not be the servant of Christ.
11 But I certify you, brethren, that the gospel which was preached of me is not after man.
12 For I neither received it of man, neither was I taught it, but by the revelation of Jesus Christ.
KJV

Many believers had to go into hiding to avoid persecution. The Romans came up with a clever way of identifying Christians. The leaders of the cities would gather all the residents and have them perform a ritual to the pagan gods of the city. Those who refused were exposed as Christians. They would be threatened with death and then asked again to perform the ritual. History tells us that many of the Christians still refused and were arrested, then martyred in the city gladiator games. Some believers were just thrown to wild animals to be devoured while the pagans cheered. Some were burned at the stakes, boiled in hot oil, or torn apart while tied to horses. They were killed in any creative deplorable way the leaders could come up with. The Christians who out of fear renounced Christ and participated in the pagan rituals to save themselves were released back into the community. Many of these believers would go back to the churches and ask for forgiveness and in many cases were allowed back into the church.

I want you to think about what was happening to the church. The strongest believers were being killed while those who were willing to compromise were left to run a spiritually depleted church. Those who walked in the Spirit with the most powerful manifestation of the power and gifts of the Holy Spirit, were being killed because they refused to deny Christ. The compromising carnal Christians were those left to run the churches. When speaking to people who exclaim that they know the church is being lead to the falling away spoken of in 2 Thess 2:3, I will sometimes smile and let them know they are 1700 years off on their proclamation. The Christian church fell away a long time ago. The revival we see today is just the gathering to bring in the harvest and proclaim the start of Christ's Kingdom.

Even through the great persecutions, by the Roman Empire, the church continued to grow. However, the depletion of the strongest believers through martyrdom left a large but weakened church with a watered-down gospel that is still prevalent even to this day. People always want to know why the gifts of the Holy Spirit seem to disappear in the history of the church starting around the time that the people taught by the apostles died off. The truth is that the Holy Spirit never left, but He only indwelled those who were really accepting the gospel of Christ. This is why you will hear the early church fathers, hundreds of years after the resurrection, still telling stories of the gifts in operation. These testimonies became less and less as the church moved farther and farther away from the truth. We can fool the pastor and one another, but no one can fool the Holy Ghost. In Revelation as Christ spoke to the Ephesus church, He warned them that He would come and remove their candlestick (Holy Spirit/angel) if they did not return to the truth.

Rev 2:4-5
4 Nevertheless I have somewhat against thee, because thou hast left thy first love.
5 Remember therefore from whence thou art fallen, and repent, and do the first works; or else I will come unto thee quickly, and **will remove thy candlestick out of his place, except thou repent.**
KJV

Tertullian, one of the greatest of the early church leaders, spoke of witnessing the gifts in operation so we know that around 200 ce the gifts were still manifesting in the church. This is around the same time that Rome began to exert control over Christianity.

In addition, around the time of Tertullian, there was a great struggle taking place in the carnal-minded Christian church, which replaced the spiritual-minded church that was left by the apostles. The tactic that the spiritual enemy was using was the same tactic used by the soothsayer Balaam while instructing king Balak of Moab on how to overcome Israel.

Balaam knew that there was no way King Balak could overcome the nation of Israel as long as they were in right relationship with God:

Num 23:7-8
7 And he took up his parable, and said, Balak the king of Moab hath brought me from Aram, out of the mountains of the east, saying, Come, curse me Jacob, and come, defy Israel.
8 **How shall I curse, whom God hath not cursed? or how shall I defy, whom the LORD hath not defied?**
KJV

No matter what the king of Moab tried, he could not overcome Israel because they were in right standing with God. Yet the same soothsayer that explained to king Balak that he could not touch Israel also gave him the strategy of how he could bring about their downfall.

Num 31:16
16 Behold, these caused the children of Israel, through **the counsel of Balaam**, to commit trespass against the LORD in the matter of Peor, and there was a plague among the congregation of the LORD.
KJV

What was the strategy that Balaam shared with king Balak on how to overcome Israel? Balaam knew the key was to get Israel to disobey God and cause a break or gap in the right relationship they had with Him. Israel's obedience allowed God's covering to be over them. **Those in right standing with God are protected from the assaults of the enemy.** They will surely come but they will not overcome you. This is what it means by "they shall surely gather, yet no weapon that is formed against you shall prosper."

Balaam instructed Balak to invite the children of Israel to a holiday festival. Israel went and participated in rituals in the celebration of Moab's pagan gods. They not only committed fornication in sexual acts with the women of Moab (sexual promiscuity was part of these celebrations), but they also committed spiritual fornication by joining in the worship of these gods. Just as Israel had feast days that God had designated as holy days, the pagan nations also had feast days to their gods.

Num 25:1-3
25:1 And Israel abode in Shittim, and the people began to commit whoredom with the daughters of Moab.
2 And **they called the people unto the sacrifices of their gods**: and **the people did eat, and bowed down to their gods**.
3 And Israel joined himself unto **Baal-peor**: and the anger of the LORD was kindled against Israel.
KJV

From ancient times, it is historically recorded that the worship of these pagan gods came with debauchery, fornications, and orgies. Sexual sins and idolatry went hand in hand. God would warn Israel repeatedly that they were not to take part in the worship of pagan gods. Baal-peor means "lord of the gap," and Israel's worship of him caused a gap between them and God.

I want you to read this warning from God to Israel very carefully:

Deut 12:29-32
29 When the LORD thy God shall cut off the nations from before thee, whither thou goest to possess them, and thou succeedest them, and dwellest in their land;
30 **Take heed to thyself that thou be not snared** by following them, after that they be destroyed from before thee; and **that thou inquire not after their gods, saying, How did these nations serve their gods? even so will I do likewise.**
31 Thou shalt not do so unto the LORD thy God: for every abomination to the LORD, which he hateth, have they done unto their gods; for even their sons and their daughters they have burnt in the fire to their gods.
32 What thing soever I command you, **observe to do it: thou shalt not add thereto, nor diminish from it.**
KJV

God gave a strong warning to Israel, not to learn the ways of the nations they were replacing in the land. He emphasized that they should not allow themselves to be snared, meaning trapped, by the practices of those nations. These wicked practices were the reason God was destroying those other nations. God did not want them to inquire after the ways of these people. **Please notice God was advising them that they are not to take the ways of the people and introduce it into worshiping Him.** You could not observe how people worshiped Saturn or any other gods and then apply these rituals in the worship of Yahweh. They were practicing all types of evil. God explained that the things the nations were doing were an abomination to Him and gave an example of them even sacrificing their children by burning them in a fire as a form of worship. He then gave the last warning that when it comes to worshiping Him they were to do **exactly** what He said. They were not to add anything to it or take anything away from it. God wanted them to worship Him exactly according to His instructions.

Any worship that we as Christians do **must be ordained by God.** The Father commands this, and Christ points out that in vain do we worship Him utilizing the commandments of men, and finally the apostles point out we are not to add or change the gospel. Brothers and sisters in Christ, the celebration of the Son of God is worship and we must do it according to what God commands, not what is invented by men.

Anytime God gives a strong warning against something, you had better believe that the enemy will be coming to try everything to get you to violate what God told you. God knew this could be used as a trap and it was what Satan used in the garden with Adam and Eve. God commanded them not to eat from the tree, and the devil disguised as a seraphim angel (serpent) did everything he could to get them to disobey (see my book **"Hidden In The Garden"**). Balaam also instructed Balak to set this same trap for Israel by inviting them to their pagan festivals. More than 1500 years later, the devil used this same trap against the early Christian church.

The last book of the Bible has a warning that was left by Christ to the early church Pergamos.

Rev 2:14
14 But I have a few things against thee, because thou hast there them that hold **the doctrine of Balaam, who taught Balac to cast a stumblingblock before the children of Israel**, to **eat things sacrificed unto idols, and to commit fornication.**
KJV

Did you notice that Christ points directly to Balaam, and what he taught Balak about how to make Israel stumble? Remember, this was Christ's message to the early church. Yet He was speaking directly to the Christian believers, not just warning them, but also exposing that those with the same mindset as Balaam had already infiltrated the church of Pergamos. Balaam's doctrine was the love of money (see the book **"The Truth About The Tithes"**), which is the reason he went with the men that Balak sent to offer him silver and gold to come and curse Israel. God told him not to leave with the men unless they returned for the second time to get him. Balaam could not wait for them to come, so he saddled up his ass and went off to meet them. The love of riches offered to him had taken a hold of his heart. This is the reason that even though God revealed to Balaam that Israel was under His protection, Balaam still devised a crafty way to ensnare Israel. He instructed Balak to invite them to the feast of the Moab gods to put them at odds with God. The cleverly set trap of Balaam was still at work in the early Christian church and we have evidence of it.

We see today how men have watered down the Gospel of Peace brought to us by our Lord and Savior Jesus (Yehoshua) Christ. This is taking place for different reasons but one of the main reasons is that the church has been infiltrated by carnal-minded leaders seeking the treasures of this world. They have put more worth in numbers than in holiness. It is more important to have the pews filled than to have people obeying God. The more people you have seated in the pews, the more money flowing into the church. If you lower the standards of holiness and present a worldly church, then the more people in the pews, which means more finances. So the devil is using these leaders in the same way he used Balaam and Balak to ensnare the people of God. We are being taught that if we compromise with the rituals of the world by partaking with the world in their celebration of their gods, that everything is ok. Christians are being led to associate with other religions such as Islam, Hinduism (yoga), Buddhism, and other pagan beliefs and religious rituals. This fight to keep the people of God away from the idolatry of the world was also present in the early church from the beginning.

1 Cor 10:14-22
14 Wherefore, my dearly beloved, **flee from idolatry**.
15 I speak as to wise men; judge ye what I say.
16 The cup of blessing which we bless, is it not the communion of the blood of Christ? The bread which we break, is it not the communion of the body of Christ?
17 For we being many are one bread, and one body: for we are all partakers of that one bread.

18 Behold Israel after the flesh: are not they which eat of the sacrifices partakers of the altar?

19 What say I then? That the idol is any thing, or that which is offered in sacrifice to idols is any thing?

20 But I say, that **the things which the Gentiles sacrifice, they sacrifice to devils, and not to God: and I would not that ye should have fellowship with devils.**

21 **Ye cannot drink the cup of the Lord, and the cup of devils: ye cannot be partakers of the Lord's table, and of the table of devils.**

22 **Do we provoke the Lord to jealousy? Are we stronger than he?**

KJV

I want to show you something. Always pay attention to when Paul says **flee** something. In verse 14 Paul warns believers to flee idolatry. **There are four things that Paul tells the believers to flee in scripture: flee fornication, flee idolatry, flee the coveting of money, and flee youthful lust. There is a reason that these things require a dire warning. Fornication (youthful lust), covetousness, and idolatry are sins that give demons access to our souls.** This goes beyond fleshly desires because fornication joins us to others and in that union any demons that have access to the fornicating collaborator now have access to us. Covetousness is the very sin that caused Adam to fall, and Paul identifies the love (covetousness) of money as the root of **ALL** evil. He says that those who fall into this trap have erred from the faith meaning they have (like Adam) fallen away. With idolatry (worshiping other gods), one has made a covenant with demons and for born-again Christians, this is actually the sin unto death that we are told not to even pray for when our brethren have fallen into it.

I know some have been taught that blaspheming the Holy Spirit is the sin unto death but this is not true. Blaspheming the Holy Spirit is the sin never forgiven so you must receive a punishment, but idolatry for those in Christ is the sin unto death. Those who have made contracts with demons before they come to Christ are not under the death penalty but need to be delivered after renouncing those false gods (demons). **These are dangerous sins because the consequences are deadly to the soul.** Ladies and gentlemen, I will be showing you further along in the book that all of these sins have strong ties that bind in Christmas.

Paul continues in verse 20 to expose the truth that the gods of the Gentiles are actually devils and demons. **He asks the believer if we can fellowship with devils, then come and have fellowship with God.** This is also, what God revealed:

Lev 17:7
7 And they shall **no more offer their sacrifices unto devils**, after whom they have gone a whoring. This shall be a statute for ever unto them throughout their generations.
KJV

This reminds me so much of Halloween when many Christian parents have their children out at night dressed as characters of the world or the kingdom of darkness, yet soon after they are in church praying for God to cover their kids. How can you expose your kids to fellowship with the devil's day, when all sorts of demons are out glorifying Satan and the things of darkness, and then want God's covering over them? We as Christians can understand the lack of knowledge of the unbelievers but we have no excuse since we know the forces of evil fellowship on this day. The day is dedicated to them. How can we have any part of this, much less allow our children to participate in it?

Satan does some things in the open, as on Halloween, and so many of us are willing to participate. Other times he hides his things through disguise and deception fooling us into participating. Our lack of knowledge causes our own downfall. If Christ told the disciples in the beginning of His ministry that they need to be wise, shouldn't we who are living at the end of the ages need to be wise also? Do we learn from the lessons of the past?

The warning that Paul left to believers of not participating in the things of this world, which brings us to eat from the devil's table, are dire warnings. Many in the early church failed to heed these warnings and it caused a great struggle in Christianity in the second, third, and fourth centuries, after Christ's death and resurrection.

In the 2nd, 3rd, and 4th centuries, Christians were being drawn into participating in the feast celebrations of pagan gods. It was like the draw to participate in the things of Satan we have today on Halloween. The church leaders understood that you could not play with the things of Satan and then tell him he cannot play. If you are using the devil's basketball, you had better believe he is going to be in the game.

Very few believers today are aware of the intense struggle that faced the early Christian church because of pagan holidays. If you are a Christian who refuses to participate in Halloween, multiply the pressure you felt initially, when you realized this was not of God, by a thousand, then you can begin to understand what our brothers and sisters in the Roman Empire were going through. Understand that not only did they have the pressure to be separate from the celebrations of the world, but they also knew that by not participating they would be identified as Christian. Once they were identified through these wicked measures, their lives were in real jeopardy.

Saturn worship is also linked to the Saturnalia of the Roman Empire, and has been camouflaged and renamed? This was done to syncretize (adopt) it into Christianity. Stephen the first martyr of the church quoted the prophet Amos who prophesied about the nation of Israel being destroyed and scattered among the heathen. The prophet Amos (Amos 5:26) was sent by God to tell the people about their evil ways and what God was going to do about their idol worship. God mentions the star that they have made to worship and calls it **"Chiun."** Notice that He points out that it is the star of their god meaning the star is a symbol of the false god. In the scripture below, Stephen, right before he was murdered by the Jewish council, recited the history of Israel and reiterated what Amos spoke from God but called the star **Remphan**. We know they are one and the same because Stephen was paraphrasing Amos:

Acts 7:43
43 Yea, ye took up the tabernacle of Moloch, and the star of your god Remphan, figures which ye made to worship them: and I will carry you away beyond Babylon.
KJV

NT:4481 Raiphan (hrahee-fan') or Rhemphan (hrem-fan'); by incorrect transliteration for a word of Hebrew origin [OT:3594]; Remphan (i.e. Kijun), **an Egyptian idol**:
KJV - Remphan. KIY'YUN (ki'un). A word occurring in the Bible only in Amos 5:26. It is generally revocalized Kaiwan or Kewan, i.e., **Saturn** (Ninib)... Rephan, evidently **the Egyptian name for Saturn.**

GODS, FALSE
Sik'kuth (si'kuth). Apparently the proper name of a star deity (Amos 5:26), rendered by ERV, RSV "Sakkuth," but in the KJV and ASV translated "tabernacle" and in the NIV "shrine"; that is, Heb. "Succoth." Interpreted as a proper name, it corresponds to **Sakkut, the Babylonian designation of the planet Saturn. The Babylonians also called the planet Saturn Kaimanu, in modernized form Kaiwanu or Kiyyun** (which see; 5:26)... See Remphan.
(from The New Unger's Bible Dictionary. Originally published by Moody Press of Chicago, Illinois. Copyright © 1988.)

Saturn the symbol of Osiris/Nimrud

What Amos called "Chiun" and Stephen called "Remphan" is no other than the planet seen in ancient times as a star, which is Saturn. What many do not realize is that this star was a representation of Osiris in the same way that the planet Venus represents Isis. Both individuals are Egyptian gods. Both Amos and Stephen were expounding on the Israelites falling into idolatry in the worship of the planet Saturn as a star, symbol of Osiris. The Saturnalia celebration of the Roman Empire is the one and the same celebration we call Christmas. The Romans worshipped Saturn as the god that gave birth to Jupiter their head god. In the same way, Osiris was worshipped as the Egyptian god that was reincarnated as Horus the sun god. The enemy of our souls has tricked many who confess the name of Christ into embracing the same pagan worship identified by Stephen as one of the main reasons God destroyed the nation of Israel and scattered the people. Let me reiterate, scripture shows that Israel's pagan worship included the planet Saturn, which they worshipped as the star of a foreign god. Sadly, we are so easily fooled. Let's examine the evidence.

Chapter 3

The Church VS The Saturnalia

Even before the birth of Christ, it was common to celebrate a midwinter feast. Among the Romans, this feast was the Saturnalia, a time when beggars were welcome at the doors of the nobleman's palace and slaves were permitted to share in all the pleasures of the master.

The probable source of the midwinter festivals among the pre-Christian cultures was the worship of the sun. It was believed that in midwinter the God of life and Light drew closest to the earth before starting once again on his Journey around it. It is known that during the days between **the seventeenth and twenty-fifth of December,** the Scandinavians, The Persians, and the Phoenicians celebrated a festival similar to the Roman Saturnalia. [Celebrations. *Becky Stevens Cordello*. Pg 160]

The big celebration in Rome was the Saturnalia. One of the greatest teachers of the early church addressed the matter of the pagan Roman feast in a thought provoking way: Please reinforce in your mind **that** he says the feast was **"commemorating some human events."** It is very important to understand that what they did (right-hand) was in remembrance (forehead) of an event.

It would follow at a consequence that we could take part in public feast, if it were proved that the public feast had nothing wrong in them and were grounded upon true views of the character of God.... However, the so-called public festivals can in no way be shown to harmonize with the service of God. Rather, on the contrary, they prove to have been **devised by men for the purpose of commemorating some human events**—or to set forth certain qualities of water, earth, or the fruits of the earth. Accordingly, it is clear that those who wish to offer an enlightened worship to the Divine Being will act according to sound reason and not take part in the public feasts. *Origen* (c. 248,E), 4.647. DECB pg 343.

Do you see that this exposes that there was now (248ce) an attempt to merge these pagan beliefs with the things of God? This point will come up again.

I want you to take a little trip in my imaginary time machine. No, you cannot keep it. I will let you borrow it for now because I want to show you something. Ok, go ahead and keep it just use it wisely. Set the dial for ancient Rome.

Picture yourself going to a feast celebration at a Roman house at the end of the seven-day celebration, long before the time of Christ. The date is different from what you know of modern times because the Julian calendar does not exist yet. What you do know is that it is taking place on the winter solstice the longest night and shortest day of the year.

When you get to the home you see the house all lit up with candles everywhere. It stands out like a great light show in the darkness of this winter's night. There are wreaths wrapped around the house pillars. The door is decorated with a circular wreath. As you enter in, you notice the fireplace is blazing because of the Yule log. In the corner of the main room in the house, there is a little evergreen tree decorated with silver and gold ornaments representing the heavenly host and presents are sitting under the tree. You see a large wooden table decorated with all types of holiday foods as the feast is about to begin. The pagan guests with holiday drinks in hand suddenly turn to you and scream out, "Merry Saturnalia!"

You get in your time machine to return to the present day and it's Christmas Dec 25. You are standing in front of your house and you see all the Christmas lights lighting up not just your house but also the whole block. You see the wreath on the door as you start to shake because of what you are beginning to realize. While reaching for the doorknob your mind is in disbelief and all you can think is, "It can't be." You open up the door and your eyes get wider and wider as you gaze around the room. You see the fireplace blazing and the Christmas tree with its silver and gold decor lit up glimmering in the room. The dining room table is overflowing with all types of foods as the season's feast is about to begin. Your family and friends turn to you with eggnog and their other favorite holiday drinks in hand and scream out, "Merry Christmas," and then you remember.

Deut 12:30-32

30 **Take heed to thyself that thou be not snared by following them**, after that they be destroyed from before thee; and that thou inquire not after their gods, saying, How did these nations serve their gods? even so will I do likewise.
31 Thou shalt not do so unto the LORD thy God: for every abomination to the LORD, which he hateth, have they done unto their gods; for even their sons and their daughters they have burnt in the fire to their gods.
32 What thing soever I command you, observe to do it: thou shalt not add thereto, nor diminish from it.
KJV

All you can say is, "Oh my God, Lord help us." Don't throw away those keys to the time machine. Before this is over we are going to go back and find out the mess we have gotten ourselves into and believe me, it is going to get a whole lot deeper.

However, for now, I want to show you how the things you do for Christmas are not as modern as you might have thought. Do you realize that Christmas rituals go back to the time of Christ (and even earlier), yet had nothing to do with Christ? Do you realize that the early church leaders were going through a desperate fight to keep these things, which will be shown to be pagan rituals, out of the church? What we have embraced today as things honoring Christ are the very things that men of God in the Body of Christ were warning believers in the church to stay away from because they were a trap, the rituals of the haters of the true God.

The quotes you are about to read are not just from anyone. These are some of the greatest voices of the early church. They were holding the battle line against the forces of evil that were threatening to overrun the church shortly after the apostles were martyred. Some of these men were bishops and elders of the churches mentioned in Revelation. There is strong evidence that Tertullian was an elder (bishop) of the perfect church Smyrna. Their voices are still talking to us today, confirming the teachings of Christ and the apostles.

WREATHS

[ADDRESSING PAGANS:] On your day of gladness, **we [Christians] neither cover our doorposts with wreaths,** nor intrude upon the day with lamps. At the call of public festivity, you consider it a proper thing to decorate your house like some new brothel.... We are accused of a lower sacrilege because we do not celebrate along with you the holidays of the Caesars in a manner forbidden alike by modesty, decency, and purity. *Tertullian* (c. 197, W), 3.44.DECB pg 342

You wanted to know where the tradition of decorating our houses for the winter season came from? Well in 197 ce Tertullian gave us the answer. It was the way of advertising the opening of a new whorehouse. Funny how it shines the light on why God did not want us to adopt pagan rituals because they glorified the very things He hated. Some would say we have taken the tradition of the brothel in a failed attempt to honor Christ. We might be ignorant of its origin but Christ is not and this is why He says we worship Him in vain through our own traditions and not as ordained by God. I have been in debates about Christmas where people justify syncretizing pagan beliefs into Christianity by trying to convince me that we can take the things of the devil and adopt them for God. **Scriptures say this is a lie**. God **specifically** says we are **not** to do this and Christ reinforced this as stated earlier.

I know that a brother was severely chastised through a vision on the very same night that his servants had wreathed his gates because of the sudden announcement of public rejoicing. Yet, he himself had neither wreathed them, nor commanded them to be wreathed.... So we are strictly judged by God in matters of this kind, even with

regard to the discipline of our family. *Tertullian* (c. 200, W) 3.71.
DECB pg 702.

LIGHTS

Is that man to be thought in his senses who present the light of candles and torches as an offering to him who is the Author and Giver of light? The light that He requires from us is of another kind…. I mean, the light of the mind, … which light no one can exhibit unless he has known God. But their gods, because they are of the earth, stand in need of lights, that they may not be in darkness. And their worshippers, because they have no taste for anything heavenly, are recalled to the earth by the very religious rites to which they are devoted. *Lactantius* (c. 304-313, W), 7.163. DECB pg 83.

Houses adorned with lights are a beautiful sight, but does God call for us to adopt this pagan tradition? Can we justify, adopting it for Christ, knowing they did it for false gods? Is God in need of us utilizing the things of the devil to give Him honor? Did He tell Israel to pick out the best things of the enemy and dedicate it to Him? **King Saul and the people in the Old Testament went up against the enemies of God to destroy them. God instructed them on exactly what to do.** I want you to pay attention to these verses below and the lesson in them:

1 Sam 15:14-15
14 And Samuel said, What meaneth then this bleating of the sheep in mine ears, and the lowing of the oxen which I hear?
15 And Saul said, They have brought them from the Amalekites: **for the people spared the best of the sheep and of the oxen, to sacrifice unto the LORD thy God; and the rest we have utterly destroyed.**
KJV

1 Sam 15:19-23
19 **Wherefore then didst thou not obey the voice of the LORD**, but didst fly upon the spoil, and didst evil in the sight of the LORD?
20 And Saul said unto Samuel, Yea, I have obeyed the voice of the LORD, and have gone the way which the LORD sent me, and have

brought Agag the king of Amalek, and have utterly destroyed the Amalekites.

21 But **the people took of the spoil, sheep and oxen, the chief of the things which should have been utterly destroyed, to sacrifice unto the LORD thy God in Gilgal.**

22 And Samuel said, Hath the LORD as great delight in burnt offerings and sacrifices, as in obeying the voice of the LORD? **Behold, to obey is better than sacrifice**, and to hearken than the fat of rams.

23 For rebellion is as the sin of witchcraft, and stubbornness is as iniquity and idolatry. Because thou hast rejected the word of the LORD, he hath also rejected thee from being king.

KJV

God was not impressed by the people taking the best of the animals of the enemy to sacrifice to Him, as Samuel pointed out. God wanted Saul and the people to obey Him.

Let's reiterate God's warning to Israel:

Deut 12:30-32

30 Take heed to thyself that thou be not snared by following them, after that they be destroyed from before thee; and that thou inquire not after their gods, saying, **How did these nations serve their gods? even so will I do likewise.**

31 **Thou shalt not do so unto the LORD thy God**: for every abomination to the LORD, which he hateth, have they done unto their gods; for even their sons and their daughters they have burnt in the fire to their gods .

32 **What thing soever I command you, observe to do it: thou shalt not add thereto, nor diminish from it.**

KJV

Let's reiterate Christ's message:

Matt 15:9

9 But **in vain they do worship me, teaching for doctrines the commandments of men.**

KJV

Matt 28:20

20 Teaching them to **observe all things whatsoever I have commanded you:** and, lo, I am with you alway, even unto the end of the world. Amen.

KJV

He says, "let your works shine." But now all our shops and gates shine! Nowadays, you will find more doors of pagans without lights and laurel wreaths than those of Christians!... **Do you say, "but the lights in front of my doors, and the wreaths on my gate-post, are an honor to God"?** However, they are not there as an honor to God, but to him who is honored **in God's place** through ceremonial observances of this kind. *Tertullian* (c. 200, w), 3.70 DECB pg 702*

More and more we are seeing that Christmas is just a copy of the Saturnalia. It is getting to the point where we can clearly see that the only difference is the name.

GIFTS:

What less of a defilement does he incur on that ground than does a business… that is publicly consecrated to an idol? The Minervalia are as much Minerva's as the Saturnalia is Saturn's. Yes, it is Saturn's day, which must necessarily be celebrated even by little slaves at the time of the Saturnalia. Likewise, New Year's gifts must be kept. And all the presents of Midwinter and the feast of Dear Kinsmanship must be exacted. The schools must be wreathed with flowers… **The same thing takes place on an idol's birthday.** Every ceremony of the devil is frequented. Who will think that these things are befitting to a Christian teacher? *Tertullian* (c. 200, W), 3.66.

MISTLETOE:

Mistletoe was hung by Druids in their temples to provide a winter refuge for the fairies and pixies while they awaited the warmth and sunshine of springtime. This feature of the Druid folklore found its way into the English Christmas festivities and was ultimately brought to America. To the Druids, mistletoe was a fertility symbol.

Ok, it is time to get back into the time machine. We have looked at some of the rituals and symbols of ancient Rome (and other nations) for their celebration of the Saturnalia. I don't think anyone can dispute the fact that these are the same things utilized in the celebration of Christmas. They are rituals taken from the celebration of other gods, which is exactly what God said we are not to do. Nevertheless, our next trip is going to take us deeper into history to clarify one of the biggest misconceptions being utilized to support the Christmas tree, which we have yet to examine. It is one of the most popular symbols, if not the most, of the Christmas season. Nothing says Christmas like a Christmas tree, and of late people have been claiming that God's dire warning about the Christmas tree in scripture is not a tree but a graven idol. Let's find out the truth. Set that time dial to 629 bce and hold on. We have an appointment with "Yah will raise" (Jeremiah).

Chapter 4

Oh Christmas Tree

Oh Christmas tree oh Christmas tree. Every year shortly after Thanksgiving, Christians (and others) go to pick up a Christmas tree to bring back home for the rest of the holiday season. It is normally a scene where all of the family pack into their vehicle and head to the local area where trees are sold. They joyfully pick out the perfect tree for their home. Others crawl up into the attic to drag out the box, which contains the old, dusty Christmas tree and its decoration ornaments. When they get the tree in place, they gather in the living room to decorate it with the ornaments. Then they all stare glary eyed as the switch is flicked on and the tree lights up the house with beautiful shimmering lights. It is a lovely sight. There is only one problem. God said, "Learn not the way of the heathen."

Your time machine arrives in 629 bce in the land of Israel. You can't even tell that it is the calm before the storm because all hell is about to break loose. God has anointed a prophet named Jeremiah to deliver His Words to the people:

Jer 1:16-17
16 And I will utter my judgments against them touching all their wickedness, **who have forsaken me, and have burned incense unto other gods, and worshipped the works of their own hands.**
17 Thou therefore gird up thy loins, and arise, and speak unto them all that I command thee: be not dismayed at their faces, lest I confound thee before them.
KJV

God is not playing and God has not changed. Sometimes because God is merciful and longsuffering, we foolishly believe that we can violate His commandments and it does not matter. Israel believed this and came up missing. God in His mercy left Judah (and Benjamin) in the land while the other 10 tribes were taken away by their enemies. Yet God has raised up Jeremiah ("raised of Yah") to send him to the remaining people in the land to speak God's Words of warning and judgment. Sadly, the people rejected what God spoke through the prophet. We are here to witness one of the warnings God gave to Israel about a ritual that they learned from the people who inhabited the land. The reason this is so important is that if we don't understand exactly what God was saying, more than 2600 years ago, then we will allow men to fool us into believing God was not saying what He said. Let's evaluate the truth in God's Words.

Jer 10:1-5
Jeremiah 10
10:1 Hear ye the word which the LORD speaketh unto you, O house of Israel:
2 Thus saith the LORD, **Learn not the way of the heathen**, and be not dismayed at the signs of heaven; for the heathen are dismayed at them.
3 For **the customs of the people are vain**: for one cutteth a tree out of the forest, the work of the hands of **the workman**, with the **axe**.
4 They **deck it with silver and with gold**; they fasten it with nails and with hammers, **that it move not**.
5 They are upright as the palm tree, but speak not: they must needs be borne, because they cannot go. Be not afraid of them; for they cannot do evil, neither also is it in them to do good.
KJV

I know many of you reading this chapter are tempted to skip over it because you have been told by many pastors, teachers, and "Facebook scholars" that the tree spoken about in Jeremiah 10 is actually a graven idol and not anything like the Christmas tree we have today. I promise you, if you take the time and carefully read this chapter, you will change your mind.

Jeremiah was given a Word that he received directly from God. He emphasized this by saying, "Thus saith the Lord." He wants the reader to know that he is repeating exactly what God has spoken to him. So what are God's first words? LEARN NOT THE WAY OF THE HEATHEN. God is saying as clear as day that His people are not to do this. We are not to adopt the ways of the wicked. It does not matter how beautiful it is, we are not to adapt the rituals of the heathen (pagans) to the things of God. God goes on to say that the customs of the people are vain. This is exactly the same thing Christ speaks to us:

Matt 15:8-9
8 This people draweth nigh unto me with their mouth, and honoureth me with their lips; but their heart is far from me.
9 But **in vain they do worship me, teaching for doctrines the commandments of men**.
KJV

Saints, there is no figuring out in this message. Christ clarifies it for us. When it comes to the worship of Christ, if we are doing something that man has come up with, then it is in vain. It is worthless worship. Too many times people try to justify something that they are doing, which is in question, by saying, "Well I am doing it to God." Where did God tell us to do it? Where did God tell you to do it? Find me the scripture that Christ or the apostles ever tell anyone to get a tree, bring it into their home, and decorate it with ornaments and lights in honor of Christ. Where? That alone disqualifies the custom. Many still practice the tree ritual and will find every excuse to do it. **However, when God tells us directly not to do it, how can we just ignore that and continue to do what we want?** Others want to justify what they do by making it seem like God did not mean what is plain in scripture. They try to give an interpretation that nullifies the truth of what is being said. I am going to prove to you through the scriptures that He is talking about what we call the Christmas tree. Just please be patient, and put aside what you think you have already learned on the subject and take this journey into understanding with me.

The Workman

God says that the people first cut a tree out of the forest and then it is worked on by a workman. First, I want to deal with your definition of workmen. I want to make it plain for you. Workman as used in Isaiah 40:19-20, Isaiah 41:7, Isaiah 44:11-12, and Jer 1:3,9 is a generic term. Just because the word is used does NOT mean the workman has to be making a graven image (statue), as many have supposed. God uses the term figuratively when He talks about scattering Judah in Zech 1:20. In Ezek. 21:31, it is used in describing men skillful in destroying. In 1 Cron 14:1, it is used to describe a carpenter building a house. In 1 Sam 13:19, it is used to describe someone making swords and spears, etc. Again, the term in Hebrew is *"charash,"* which just means a skilled worker of any form, and not someone who specifically works with graven images. Just because this word is used in Jer 10: 3, does not mean the workman is working on a graven image and not a pagan parallel to today's Christmas Tree.

God often addresses workmen making images in scripture. Some people would have you believe that all God did was address images, but that is not true. God addressed the trees (groves) also.

Isa 17:8
8 And he shall not look to the altars, the work of his hands, neither shall respect that which his fingers have made, either **the groves**, or the images.

2 Chron 34:7
7 And when he had broken down the altars and **the groves**, and had beaten the graven images into powder, and cut down all the idols throughout all the land of Israel, he returned to Jerusalem.

Now some might ask the question of why you would need a workman to cut down a Christmas tree. How many people know that the Christmas tree you buy at Wal-Mart or Publix is not what you get if you planted a seed of the same tree in your backyard? The natural trees are shaped similar but they are shaped and pruned as they grow to take on a perfect pyramid shape. The trees today also get a once-over before they are packaged, given mounts, and sold. This is not new; this was done in the same manner in ancient times.

People who prune and shape these trees as they grow are skilled in the knowledge of what has to be cut off the tree to obtain the triangle shape needed to form a Christmas tree. They are skillful workmen. If all this has to be done now, when everybody can drive down to Wal-Mart or Home Depot and buy tools, what about ancient times? Tools were a novelty in those days and mostly those who used them by trade possessed them.

Another important point in Jer 10:3 is the tool used on the tree. The **ax** is not what you think it is. This tool is not used to cut the tree down but to prune the tree. Why are you going to prune a tree that you are going to chop up, carve, and burn in the fire to make an idol?

TOOLS

Ax. A cutting and chopping tool. Eight different Hebrew words and one Greek word are translated ax in English versions of the Bible. Several of these axes were tools designed for specific jobs. **One type of ax was a sort of pruning tool (Jer 10:3)** with a curved blade...

65

(from Nelson's Illustrated Bible Dictionary, Copyright (c)1986, Thomas Nelson Publishers)

Again, why prune a tree you're going to make into a graven image? When I say graven image, I am talking about the ancient practice of chopping down a tree, cutting off a block section that is carved into a statue, and then overlay it with gold and silver as a figurine to worship as a god.

Now some have pointed out that in context, Isaiah 40:19-20, Isaiah 41:7, Isaiah 44:11-12, and Jer 1:3, 9 are telling the same story of a graven image being made. Yet I want to point out the inaccuracies. First, let's deal with "deck it with silver and with gold." You see that word "deck" I want to get this clear, it is NEVER used to describe a graven image. The word is *"Yaphah"* in Hebrew, which is closely associated with *"Yapheh"* in Hebrew and it has nothing to do with putting gold or silver on wood to make an image or idol. In scripture, it is never associated with gold or silver covered graven images. The plain meaning is to make fair (beautiful); the wisdom of God is so wonderful. Sometimes we forget that in Jer 10:1-5, it was God speaking directly to Israel.

God used a word that actually identifies what the tree is, but He did it in a way that only the Holy Spirit could reveal.

OT:3302
yaphah (yaw-faw'); a primitive root; properly, **to be bright**, i.e. (by implication) beautiful:
KJV - be beautiful, be (makeself) **fair** (-r), **deck**.
(Biblesoft's New Exhaustive Strong's Numbers and Concordance with Expanded Greek-Hebrew Dictionary. Copyright (c) 1994, Biblesoft and International Bible Translators, Inc.)

The word "yaphah" is also translated as FAIR, it is translated as DECK in Jer 10. It is only used in the Bible to describe **two things**.

The first thing is a woman being beautified.

Jer 4:30
30 And when thou art spoiled, what wilt thou do? Though thou clothest thyself with crimson, though thou deckest thee **with ornaments of gold**, though thou rentest thy face with painting, in vain shalt thou make thyself **fair**; thy lovers will despise thee, they will seek thy life.

God is describing a woman making herself beautiful. He uses fair (deck 3302), not the first deck you see in the verse (Jer 4:30) but the word later meaning fair. She is putting on gold ornaments. In Jer 10, no goldsmith is mentioned because He is describing putting on ornaments. **God uses 3302 (strongs # deck, fair)** because this is the word used to beautify by putting on ornaments. The word is never used to describe putting gold on a graven image by a goldsmith. Those who would have you believe that this is an idol will quote several places in the book of Isaiah where it talks about workman and graven images or idols. However, notice that no goldsmith is mentioned in Jer 10 and yet they are mentioned in Isaiah.

The second thing is a TREE beautified.

Ezek 31:7-8
7 THUS WAS HE **FAIR** in his greatness, in the length of his branches: for his root was by great waters.
8 The cedars in the garden of God could not hide him: the fir trees were not like his boughs, and the chestnut trees were not like his branches; nor any tree in the garden of God was like unto him in his beauty.

I want you to understand that God used specific words to make sure that this could not be mistaken as an idol. God knew what people would try to do. He knew they would try to twist the scriptures to show believers that this was not a tree. He used a word that is only used for women and trees and is associated with putting on ornaments. He wanted those who would take the time to research the words to have no doubt of exactly what He was talking about. Glory be to God! And look how He uses "*Yaheh,*" the other word associated with "yaphah":

Ezek 31:3
3 Behold, the Assyrian was a cedar in Lebanon with **fair** branches, and with a shadowing shroud, and of an high stature; and his top was among the thick boughs.

Ezek 31:9
9 I have made him **fair** by the multitude of **his branches**: so that all the trees of Eden, that were in the garden of God, envied him.

Jer 11:16
16 The Lord called thy name, A green olive tree, **fair**, and of goodly fruit: with the noise of a great tumult he hath kindled fire upon it, and the **branches** of it are broken.

Notice that nothing is said above about the tree being made into a graven Image. All are about the tree itself being beautiful, which is in context with Jer 10: 3-5 where nothing is said about melting gold by a gold-smith and applying it as a covering to an idol.

You can also find these two words associated with a woman putting on ornaments like earrings, necklace, bracelets, etc. Once again, it is NEVER associated with putting gold and silver on a graven image.

Those who have researched the real origin of the Christmas tree probably have caught on to why I said this was such wisdom. The tree is really a symbol of Asherah (Astarte or Ashtoreth), the queen of heaven. In ancient times, there were altars set up in Canaan (and other places) to honor pagan gods. As stated earlier, we understand that the small tree or grove placed next to the altar of Baal (and El) represents Asherah his consort the goddess of fertility. These were small trees, called groves, which were evergreen (meaning they stayed green throughout the year). If what I am saying is correct, there should be some example of ornaments being applied to the grove (evergreen trees) also.

2 Kings 23:7
7 And he brake down the houses of the sodomites, that were by the house of the Lord, where **the women wove hangings for the grove.**

In the worship of the pagan god Baal, there were items made to hang on the small trees. If you do a study of the items hung on these groves or small trees, you will find that 2000 years before Christ these trees were beautified with gold and silver balls as ornaments representing the heavenly host (stars, sun, moon, planets) and other woven hangings.

Some have the false belief that these were poles and that's how they come up with the totem poles, but this is not true. Jewish scholars have argued for years that the word "Asherah" should not be translated poles but small tree.

That it moves not:

Jer 10:4
4 They deck it with silver and with gold; they fasten it with nails and with hammers, **that it move not.**
KJV

Ok, let's now deal with the "THAT IT MOVE NOT." Scholars have said that this term links Isaiah 40:20, 41:7, and Jer 10:4 together and since the other scriptures are talking about a graven image, Jer 10:4 is also.

Isa 40:20
20 He that is so impoverished that he hath no oblation chooseth a tree that will not rot; he seeketh unto him a cunning workman to prepare a graven image, **that shall not be moved.**
KJV

Isa 41:7
7 So the carpenter encouraged the goldsmith, and he that smootheth with the hammer him that smote the anvil, saying, It is ready for the sodering: and he fastened it with nails, **that it should not be moved.**
KJV

At first glance, does this really make sense? If you take a simple look at it, it would seem so. However, when you look in-depth into the Hebrew, you find it is not. In Isaiah 40 and 41 the Hebrew word used is *"Mowt."* The word *mowt* has different meanings but in Isaiah, it implies being moved. Both scriptures are describing nailing down an item in preparation to work on it. In Isaiah 40:20 it says, "Prepare," in Isaiah 41:7 it says, "It is ready." After those words are stated, the nails are applied. Now if these people are right that in Jer 10: 3-5 it's the same thing, then we should find the same word or a similar word used in Isaiah with graven images.

So what do we find? No such thing, "*Puwq*" is the word used in Jeremiah 10: 3-5, and even though it is translated there as "move" in English, in the Hebrew it has a different meaning than in Isaiah (40, 41). "*Puwq*" in Hebrew means "stumble" (topple over). That has nothing to do with the soldering process of making a statue or image. "*Puwq*" is only used in the Bible twice but look at the other verse.

Isa 28:7
7 But they also have erred through wine, and through strong drink are out of the way; the priest and the prophet have erred through strong drink, they are swallowed up of wine, they are out of the way through strong drink; they err in vision, **they stumble** in judgment.

What would seem to be identical in Jeremiah and the verses of Isaiah, have very little correlation when you look into the Hebrew. Jer 10: 3-5 is talking about a tree toppling over (stumbling), the scriptures in Isaiah (40, 41) are talking about an idol being nailed down so it won't be moved or shaken during the creation process. So let's go back and look at why they nailed down the statue.

Isa 41:7
7 So the carpenter encouraged the goldsmith, and he that smootheth with the hammer him that smote the anvil, saying, **It is ready for the sodering**: and he fastened it with nails, that it should not be moved.

We see they are nailing down the statue to start the process of applying the gold with hammer and anvil.

Now let's look at Jeremiah.

Jer 10:4
4 They **deck it with silver and with gold; they fasten it with nails and with hammers, that it move not.**

Did you notice the gold and silver (ornaments) are applied first and then the tree is nailed down? The tree decorated and then nailed down vs. a statue nailed down to apply gold by soldering and hammering it to form. We have already discussed that the word here for "deck" in Hebrew means, "To beautify" and is associated with putting on ornaments, not with soldering. In addition, we note that *Mowt* is the word always used when describing a graven image not being moved in the process of it being made, which is not in Jer 10: 3-5. In Jer 10 the word is *puwq,* which is never used concerning a graven image. The putting on of the silver and gold before it is nailed down means it is not part of the molding process. It does not match the steps used in making an idol. Why not? Because it is not an idol, it is a tree nailed to stand up-right without falling. It is just like the Christmas tree.

Let me reiterate that what is being described in Jer 10: 3-5 is not the soldering of gold and silver to a piece of a tree that has been cut, burned, carved, or nailed down so it won't move out of place, and soldered with gold and silver. Jer 10: 3-5 is describing cutting down a tree from the forest, pruning it, bringing it into the house, and decorating it with gold and silver. Then it is nailed in place so it won't topple over. It is described according to how it looks.

Jer 10:5
5 They are **upright as the palm tree**, but speak not: they must needs be borne, because they cannot go. Be not afraid of them; for they cannot do evil, neither also is it in them to do good.

Isiaih 40:19-20 talks about making a small statue from wood and covering it with gold.

Do the research. Look up the graven images that were in people's houses. They were statues, not great big statues but little statues. Only kings had the means to make large statues; the everyday worshipers made little statues, which they placed in their homes. Example:

Gen 31:19
19 And Laban went to shear his sheep: and Rachel had stolen the **images** that were her father's.

No one knew Rachel had stolen the images. Can you picture Rachel dragging these big totem pole like structures down the street and no one seeing it? The reason no one saw the items is because the images were small enough for a woman to carry in her hands concealed. Is this something you nail down so that it will not topple over (*Puwq*)? Absolutely not! Is this something that stands upright like a palm tree? Absolutely not!

In addition, let me also add why God used the word upright like a palm tree.

Judg 20:33
33 And all the men of Israel rose up out of their place, and put themselves in array at **Baal-tamar**: and the liers in wait of Israel came forth out of their places, even out of the meadows of Gibeah.

You see the word Baal-tamar? It means "Lord of the palm trees." Palm trees were worshipped in Egypt and parts of Israel already. God gave an example so that people would know that these trees were being worshiped in the same manner.

I also want to clear up a couple other things.

Notice in verse 8 "the stock" is the same Hebrew word translated "tree" (Strong's concordance #6086) as in verse 3. It should be translated "the tree is a doctrine of vanities." This information is for those who have been wrongly taught that this is a tree carved into a wooden image and overladen with gold and silver. Although this took place in the Old Testament, this is not what is being spoken of here. This is also reinforced by the wrong application of verse 8 and 9 of Jer 10.

Jer 10:8-9
8 But they are altogether brutish and foolish: the stock is a doctrine of vanities.
9 **Silver spread into plates is brought from Tarshish, and gold from Uphaz, the work of the workman, and of the hands of the founder: blue and purple is their clothing: they are all the work of cunning men.**

It is easy to misinterpret the silver and gold from verse 9 as being applied to the stock (that should have been translated tree) of verse 8, which would give you a false picture of a carved image overlaid with silver and gold. The truth be told, the silver and gold plates were **to be cut into wires to decorate the fine purple linen** of verse 9 for the priests of these false religions' garments. Compare with:

Ex 39:2-3
2 And he made the ephod of gold, blue, and purple, and scarlet, and fine twined linen.
3 And **they did beat the gold into thin plates, and cut it into wires, to work it in the blue, and in the purple, and in the scarlet, and in the fine linen, with cunning work.**

I think it has been easily shown that this was not a tree being processed into a statue image. This was just as God said, a tree taken from the forest, pruned, gold and silver put on to beautify it, then nailed down so it wouldn't topple over, and it stood upright like a palm tree.

Please saints, let no one deceive you on this matter. God knew why He gave this warning, and it was not just for Israel. Think about it, you have millions of people in this country and billions all over the world that will not set foot in a church but have a Christmas tree up in their homes. Why? If it is of God, the world wants nothing to do with it. So why do they so warmly embrace the Christmas tree? **All over America, they talk about the separation of church and state to the point that the Ten Commandments have been removed out of government buildings.** If the Christmas tree represents Christ, then why does every government building have them? Isn't that a violation of the separation of church and state?

The world, which wants nothing to do with the things of God, know what many Christians refuse to accept that the Christmas tree has nothing to do with the God of the Bible. Show me in the scriptures where anyone tells us to put up a tree in worship or celebration of Christ. Christ said if we are worshiping according to what men teach, then it is in vain.

We now have a deeper understanding of the tree of Jer 10 and proof that it was not an idol or statue but an actual decorated tree. I want to take you a lot deeper into the knowledge and the symbolism of the tree. I want you to understand why it is linked to a goddess and why God hates it. Crank up the time machine and get ready to be introduced to another prophet. God will strengthen! Can you feel that vibration? I think the time machine is running a little hot. Set course for 583 bce. Wintertime.

Chapter 5

Unholy Night

It was the night before Christmas and all through the temple... We touch down around 583 bce in Judea. It is the day before the winter solstice. The winter solstice is the shortest day (least amount of daylight) of the year in the northern hemisphere according to the cycle of the sun. The solstice moves on a 26,000-year cycle, and in 583 bce the shortest day of the year fell on December 25th. We are right on time because the prophet Ezekiel is about to have an out-of-body experience with the angel of the Lord, whom God will be speaking through. We are not only going to watch the interaction between God and Ezekiel but will also tap into the vision that God is going to show him about what is taking place in the temple at Jerusalem. The priests think God does not see what they are doing. God is going to reveal their abominations for the whole world to see. My job is to help you see what God is showing and explain the meaning of the abominations.

It was the sixth year, the sixth month, and the fifth day of the month. Ezekiel was meeting with tribal elders at his home when God showed up. He was lifted up by a lock of his hair and taken in a vision to Jerusalem.

Ezek 8:1-2
8:1 And it came to pass in the sixth year, in the sixth month, in the fifth day of the month, as I sat in mine house, and the elders of Judah sat before me, that the hand of the Lord GOD fell there upon me.

2 Then I beheld, and lo a likeness as the appearance of fire: from the appearance of his loins even downward, fire; and from his loins even upward, as the appearance of brightness, as the colour of amber.
KJV

God wanted to show Ezekiel the abominations that were taking place in His temple. The first thing He showed him was an image of jealousy that was placed at the northern gates by the altar. Think about the importance of God literally pointing out to the prophet what Ezekiel identified as the image of jealousy.

Ezek 8:5-6
5 Then said he unto me, Son of man, lift up thine eyes now the way toward the north. So I lifted up mine eyes the way toward the north, and behold northward **at the gate of the altar this image of jealousy in the entry.**
6 He said furthermore unto me, Son of man, seest thou what they do? even the great abominations that the house of Israel committeth here, that I should go far off from my sanctuary? but turn thee yet again, and thou shalt see greater abominations.
KJV

The question that remains is, "What was it?" What was the thing that God called an abomination? The key to understanding what God pointed out is realizing that it was located by the altar. Every time Israel fell into apostasy (Baal worship), they set up an altar to Baal with something specific next to it. When God anointed Gideon to be a judge over His people, the first command He gave Gideon was to destroy the altar of Baal and **the grove** that was planted next to it.

Judg 6:25-26
25 And it came to pass the same night, that the LORD said unto him, Take thy father's young bullock, even the second bullock of seven years old, and throw down **the altar of Baal** that thy father hath, and **cut down the grove** that is by it:
26 And build an altar unto the LORD thy God upon the top of this rock, in the ordered place, and take the second bullock, and offer a burnt sacrifice with **the wood of the grove which thou shalt cut down.** KJV

God spoke to Gideon and told him to cut down the grove and use the wood to make a fire. From this, we know that the grove was a tree. Archeologists would find small logs buried next to ancient sites that were found to contain the remains of altars to the pagan god Baal. He was worshipped by the Canaanites who occupied the land of Israel before the Israelites got there. Afterwards, the Israelites themselves would fall into apostasy and embrace the worship of this false god. The small logs were the remains of small evergreen trees that were planted by the altars of Baal. This is confirmed by a warning that Moses gave to the Israelites before they entered the land of Canaan.

Deut 16:21
21 Thou shalt not plant thee **a grove of any trees** near unto the altar of the LORD thy God, which thou shalt make thee.
KJV

We saw earlier where God warned Israel that when they came into the land they were not to learn the traditions, rituals, and practices of the people they were supplanting. This is why Moses gave them a commandment not to plant a grove of any trees next to God's altar. God was not going to allow His altar to have groves next to it like the false god Baal.

The tree represents Asherah the consort (wife) of Baal, which was also worshiped as the queen of heaven. Now we can fully understand why God was using words for the tree in Jer 10, which also could be applied to a woman putting on ornaments (earrings). The tree symbolized a goddess, the wife of Baal. Archeologists have also found evidence of Israel attempting to add Asherah to the worship of Yahweh (God). Her name and figurines have been found in places where Yahweh was worshipped, confirming the apostasy mentioned in the scriptures. We know this was apostasy because God forbade Israel from building any altars (on their own accord) away from the tabernacle, and later the temple. The artifacts that were found have come from places where God did not allow worship. This confirms that the people had mixed the worship of Asherah as the grove with the worship of the true God.

When God points out the abomination in the temple courtyard next to the altar, it is apparent that this was a grove (small tree). However, is there any indication in the scriptures that confirm that a grove was placed in the temple? Let's look at a testimony from the life of King Manasseh, who scripture indicates was the most wicked king to rule over Judah:

2 Kings 21:3-7
3 For he built up again the high places which Hezekiah his father had destroyed; and **he reared up altars for Baal, and made a grove**, as did Ahab king of Israel; and worshipped all **the host of heaven**, and served them.
4 And he built altars in the house of the LORD, of which the LORD said, in Jerusalem will I put my name.
5 And **he built altars for all the host of heaven** in the two courts of the house of the LORD.
6 And he made his son pass through the fire, and observed times, and used enchantments, and dealt with familiar spirits and wizards: he wrought much wickedness in the sight of the LORD, to provoke him to anger.
7 And **he set a graven image of the grove that he had made in the house,** of which the LORD said to David, and to Solomon his son, In this house, and in Jerusalem, which I have chosen out of all tribes of Israel, will I put my name for ever:
KJV

Now we have the evidence that this grove or an image of it, was brought into the temple. This also emphasizes that these trees were called images even though they were not statues. Did you notice that it says Manasseh also worshiped the host of heaven? What was the host of heaven?

Deut 4:19
19 And lest thou lift up thine eyes unto heaven, and when thou seest **the sun, and the moon, and the stars, even all the host of heaven,** shouldest be driven to **worship them, and serve them,** which the LORD thy God hath divided unto all nations under the whole heaven.
KJV

The host of heaven is identified as the sun, moon, and stars that the people were worshiping, along with Baal and the grove (Asherah). For those who are still trying to hold on to the false belief that the tree being spoken of by God in Jer 10 is a statue, did you notice that God also pointed out the heavens with the worship of the tree? God said the host of heaven are for signs.

Jer 10:2
2 Thus saith the LORD, Learn not the way of the heathen, and be not dismayed **at the signs of heaven**; for the heathen are dismayed at them.
KJV

The grove, which God called the image of jealousy that was positioned next to the altar of God, was also tied into the worship of heavenly bodies. The stars, moon, and sun were part of the worship of the grove and this too is verification that items were hung on these trees representing heavenly bodies, remember:

2 Kings 23:7
7 And he brake down the houses of the sodomites, that were by the house of the LORD, where the women wove **hangings for the grove.**
KJV

I remember many years ago when I was initially doing my research on Christmas, I came across a picture of a hieroglyph that showed Egyptians hanging round orbs on a little tree. Since then I have come across many Egyptian hieroglyphs of trees that have been located in places of worship being decorated by and for their gods.

Remember, Asherah was worshiped as the queen of heaven so she was the queen of the heavenly hosts. This explains why the ancients would hang images of suns, moons, and stars on the tree that represented Asherah. It is the same thing we see being done today in the decoration of the Christmas trees.

The early church father's made mention of these trees:
We wish to hear from or learn from you something befitting the gods. However, on the contrary, you bring forward to us the cutting

off of breast, the lopping off of men's members, ragings, blood, frenzies, the self-destruction of maidens, and flowers **and trees that spring up from the blood of the dead!"** *Arnobius* (c. 305, E) 6.495 DECB 316*

What Arnobius was referring to was the pagan rituals to include the tree that sprung up from the blood of Nimrod (Osiris). Nimrod was the grandson of Noah, who was the first man-king worshiped by the people as a god. He is believed to be, by most sources, the same Osiris, the first pharaoh of Egypt. The record of his death from the book of the dead (Egyptian scriptures) shows he was torn to pieces by giants. His wife Isis took his phallus (genitalia) and buried it by a tree stump. The next day when she came back to the site where she buried the body part, she finds a small evergreen tree has grown and a young boy is under the tree, which she says is the reincarnated Osiris (Nimrod). This legend is actually where the tradition of presents under the Christmas tree really comes from. She names the boy Horus, who we know today as the Egyptian sky god. Specifically, his right eye was considered a symbol for the sun and his left the symbol for the moon.

I have noticed in recent years that there is a movement by scholars to morph the legend of Horus by changing the story subtly so it resembles the story of Christ. It is an attempt to say that the story of Christ is taken from myths but research into what the Bible actually says shows it is not.

Most cultures have adapted the Nimrod story, in some form, into their religious beliefs. They give different names to their gods, such as Odin, Baal, Tammuz, Horus, Apollo, and so on. When you research into their attributes, it exposes that these gods are all linked to Nimrod in some way. The Egyptian myth, of Horus being reincarnated under a small tree, is also an adaptation of the Nimrod and Semiramis (his wife) story.

GODS, PAGAN
The ancient Babylonian and Assyrian goddess Ishtar symbolized Mother Earth in the natural cycles of fertility on earth. Many myths grew up around this female deity. She was the goddess of love, so the practice of ritual prostitution became widespread in the fertility cult

dedicated to her name. Temples to Ishtar had many priestesses, or sacred prostitutes, who symbolically acted out the fertility rites of the cycle of nature. Ishtar has been identified with the Phoenician Astarte, the Semitic Ashtoreth, and the Sumerian Inanna. Strong similarities also exist between Ishtar and the Egyptian Isis, the Greek Aphrodite, and the Roman Venus.

Associated with Ishtar was the young god **Tammuz**, considered both divine and mortal (Ezek 8:14). In Babylonian mythology **Tammuz died annually and was reborn year after year**, representing the yearly cycle of the seasons and the crops. This pagan belief later was identified with the pagan gods Baal and Anat in Canaan.
(Nelson's Illustrated Bible Dictionary, Copyright (c)1986, Thomas Nelson Publishers)

The Sumerians, who predate the Egyptians, also had tree worship. What is more shocking is the fact that the Sumerian version had an angel (spirit) sitting at the top. In the same fashion, we see many Christmas trees with an angel on top. These rituals predate Christ's birth by thousands of years. This is not a coincidence; these are rituals and traditions passed down through the generations that show these forms of worship have a common source. **What all these people have in common is that they are not worshiping the Creator of the universe but rather false gods that represent devils and demons.**

The early church fathers testified of these traditions in their apologetic writings against the pagans. These disputes were taking place in the third and fourth generations after Christ's ascension. This is the same time-period when the great persecutions were taking place by the Roman Empire against the church.

"For the initiated, the **"holy night"** is the telltale of the rites of licentiousness. The glare of torches reveals vicious indulgences…. The fire does not dissemble. Rather, it exposes and punishes what it is requested. Such are the mysteries of the atheists. I call them atheist for good reason. For they do not know the true God, and they pay shameless worship to **a boy torn in pieces by the Titans.** *Clement of Alexandria* (c. 195, e), 2.177"DECB 469

In Egypt, there are sacred rites in honor of Isis, since she either lost or found her little son. At first, her priest (having made their bodies smooth) beat their breasts and **lament-as the goddess herself had done when her child was lost.** Afterwards, the boy is brought forward, as if found, and their mourning is changed into joy. *Lactantius* (c. 304-313, W) DECB 701*

"The sacred rites of the Eleusinian Ceres are not unlike those [of Isis]. For just as in those **(where the boy Osiris is sought with the wailing of his mother),** so likewise in these, Proserpine is carried away to contract an incestuous marriage with her uncle.... Her sacred rites are celebrated with the throwing of torches. *Lactanius* (c.304-313, w) 7.35"*DECB 469

Notice that the worship of Osiris (and Tammuz) as indicated by the early church fathers was accompanied by crying and wailing in remembrance of his death. This annual ritual took place the night before his birthday. For Tammuz, the crying took place on the day of his death in the beginning of July (summer solstice) and right before the winter solstice the night before his rebirth. The Holy Night mentioned by Clement of Alexandria was the longest night of the year, which took place before the winter solstice. The winter solstice in the time of Ezekiel fell on December 25th. This identifies the exact night that Ezekiel was shown the temple in the vision. What God was showing the prophet was the worship of Tammuz.

Ezek 8:14-15
14 Then he brought me to the door of the gate of the LORD's house which was toward the north; and, behold, there sat women **weeping for Tammuz.**
15 Then said he unto me, Hast thou seen this, O son of man? turn thee yet again, and thou shalt see greater abominations than these.

God showed Ezekiel the women weeping for Tammuz, mimicking what Isis did the night before Osiris was reincarnated as Horus. The early church leaders testified of this wailing of Isis and her followers. It was in the same way that the priests in Egypt would cry and wail until the sun rose in the morning, then a small boy would be brought out symbolizing the birth of the new sun. God then explains that Ezekiel is about to see an even worst abomination than that:

Ezek 8:16-18
16 And he brought me into the inner court of the LORD's house, and, behold, at the door of the temple of the LORD, between the porch and the altar, were about five and twenty men, with their backs

toward the temple of the LORD, and their **faces toward the east; and they worshipped the sun toward the east.**

17 Then he said unto me, Hast thou seen this, O son of man? Is it a light thing to the house of Judah that they commit the abominations which they commit here? for they have filled the land with violence, and have returned to provoke me to anger: and, lo, they put the branch to their nose.

18 Therefore will I also deal in fury: mine eye shall not spare, neither will I have pity: and though they cry in mine ears with a loud voice, yet will I not hear them.

KJV

The worst of the abominations was the worship of the sun, which would have started the next morning. We call this day December 25th because it was the winter solstice but the time machine took us back long before the Julian calendar even existed. **There was no December 25th in 583 bce, there was only the sixth year, the sixth month, and the sixth day of the month.** The birthday of the sun, whose worship is an abomination to God.

Job 31:26-28

26 If I **beheld the sun when it shined,** or the moon walking in brightness;

27 And **my heart hath been secretly enticed,** or my mouth hath kissed my hand:

28 **This also were an iniquity to be punished by the judge: for I should have denied the God that is above.**

KJV

For anyone to believe there is no link between those ancient rituals and what we do today is pure self-retained ignorance. **The truth is in the Word of God for everyone to see, but we have to want to know the truth. When we refuse the truth, we are left in bondage and sadly, many still don't realize this.**

You think you have heard the worst of this but it gets significantly worse. Sometimes we are so shaken that we just do not want to hear any more. Nevertheless, we have to because we need to hear the whole truth even if it cracks the foundation of what we believe. If a house is built on sand, eventually it will crumble back into the sea. It is better to have the house crumble now and rebuilt on solid ground with the knowledge of the truth than to have the house crumble when we stand before God.

How bad can it get? Take some time and gather your composure before we go any further. We are headed to a place of understanding that very few people have journeyed. If God isn't with you, it's going to be hard to believe what you're about to be shown. **Yes, I am going to show and prove that Christmas is the mark of the beast. This is going to be a riveting but necessary journey.**

Christmas and the Mark of the Beast

Chapter 6

Israel's Mark from God

I know, I know, I know... all of your life you have been told that the mark of the beast is a computer chip that will be placed in your right hand or in your forehead. This has been preached in countless number of churches in modern times. As technologies have gotten better and microchips have gotten smaller, the churches has gone full speed ahead with this understanding. The biggest problem with this is that God also placed a mark on the right hand and forehead of Israel. If Israel's mark was not a computer chip, then the beast's, which is a counterfeit to Israel's, is not either.

God likes to hide things in plain sight to confound the wicked. It is amazing how we can read a scripture repeatedly and never see a revelation that is in plain sight. The Holy Spirit can then take us to the same scripture, and before we are even finished reading we are praising God.

Over the years, I have noticed that certain words in the Bible can be translated from Hebrew into different English words (same in the Greek). One example of this is the Hebrew word **"Owth,"** which is translated into English as token, mark, sign, or miracle. These four words seem similar yet can have different meanings in English. Remember, they all come from the same Hebrew word. If you're looking through the Bible for the answer to a question with the word "mark" and you run across a verse with the word "token," it is easy to disregard it. I want you to look at these three verses, which are the first three times that Owth is used in the Bible, to clarify what I am saying:

Gen 1:14
14 And God said, Let there be lights in the firmament of the heaven to divide the day from the night; and let them be for **signs**, and for seasons, and for days, and years:
KJV

Gen 4:15
15 And the LORD said unto him, Therefore whosoever slayeth Cain, vengeance shall be taken on him sevenfold. And the LORD set **a mark** upon Cain, lest any finding him should kill him.
KJV

Gen 9:12
12 And God said, This is the **token** of the covenant which I make between me and you and every living creature that is with you, for perpetual generations:
KJV

Sign, mark, or token can take the understanding of the reader into different directions depending on which word is used. One is the sun and moon being signs, one is a mark on a man, and the other is the token of a rainbow. When you also add in the metaphoric nature of the Bible, it is easy to miss the understanding. You need to link verses together to get a deeper meaning or it can get confusing.

When I ask believers if they know that God gave Israel a mark that He put on their right hand and on their forehead they look at me perplexed. If they do not even know that God gave a mark on the right hand and forehead of His people, they are not going to be able to link it to the beast's mark. If they cannot link it to the beast's mark, then they will not realize that it actually opens up the understanding of what the beast's mark really is. If they cannot put those pieces together, they will continue to read the scripture that shows the meaning of the beast's mark and never see it.

Deut 6:6-8
6 And these words, which I command thee this day, shall be in thine heart:
7 And thou shalt teach them diligently unto thy children, and shalt talk of them when thou sittest in thine house, and when thou walkest by the way, and when thou liest down, and when thou risest up.
8 And thou shalt bind them for **a sign upon thine hand**, and they shall be **as frontlets between thine eyes**.

After initially reading the verses above, it would seem as if Moses is saying God is going to write His words on Israel's hand and between the frontlets of their eyes (forehead). What I want you to understand is that this is a dark saying (allegory), nothing is being written on the hand or the forehead. **Your hand and forehead are metaphors.** This is why not comprehending the metaphor will cause you to miss the understanding and believe that the mark is a computer chip. I call this "lost in the metaphor." (I teach this in-depth in my book "Lost In The Metaphor.") **Your right hand is something you do (your actions) and the mark on your forehead means in remembrance.** God was saying to speak His Words continuously so they would remember.

Let's look at another scripture describing the mark:

Ex 13:15-16
15 And it came to pass, when Pharaoh would hardly let us go, that the LORD slew all the firstborn in the land of Egypt, both the firstborn of man, and the firstborn of beast: **therefore I sacrifice to the LORD all that openeth the matrix,** being males; but all the firstborn of my children I redeem.
16 And **it shall be for a token upon thine hand, and for frontlets between thine eyes:** for by strength of hand the LORD brought us forth out of Egypt.

Here we have Moses speaking to the Israelites about what took place in Egypt. He is imploring the people to remember when they were being held by Pharaoh who refused to let them go. The Lord, our God, slew the firstborn of men and beast, which caused Pharaoh to release Israel. He is showing that this is the reason they sacrifice the firstborn of all males that open the matrix (womb) of all their animals and redeem their children (so they don't have to sacrifice them). The translation says **token** and not mark, then **frontlets** and not forehead. This is why so many have missed what Moses is revealing and how it ties into the devil's mark. Token is a mark, and frontlets mean the forehead.

towphaphah
OT:2903 towphaphah (to-faw-faw'); from an unused root meaning to go around or bind; **a fillet for the forehead:**

KJV - **frontlet.**
(Biblesoft's New Exhaustive Strong's Numbers and Concordance with Expanded Greek-Hebrew Dictionary. Copyright © 1994, 2003 Biblesoft, Inc. and International Bible Translators, Inc.)

There is nothing to write on the right hand and forehead. Sacrificing animals and redeeming children are not a written mark. **These rituals cannot be put on the right-hand or forehead so this alone allows us to recognize that the right hand and forehead are metaphors with a hidden meaning.** When we are lost in a metaphor, it is like being in a maze where we cannot find our way out to receive the correct understanding. Let's work our way through the metaphor.

God wanted the people to remember what happened to them in Egypt. The ritual they did continually in their traditions was so they would always remember what happened. Every time a child would ask their parents why they do the sacrifices, the parents would tell them, "We do this sacrifice to remember when and how God took us out of Egypt." The mark is a ritual that you do (right-hand), in remembrance of (forehead). We are no longer lost in the metaphor. **The mark on your right hand is what you do. The mark on your forehead means in remembrance of.** This is the key of understanding, which opens up the knowledge locked away in the metaphor. You may now exit the maze.

Chapter 7

The Mark of the Beast Revealed

Please understand that there is going to be a fight to get you to reject what is about to be revealed to you. It is going to go against what you have been taught, and for most reading this book, it is going to hit hard against a tradition that you hold very dear. Nevertheless, it is the unadulterated truth. For some, there will be demonic forces around you trying to convince you to reject the truth. A few individuals will hear voices in their heads saying, "This is a lie, don't believe what he is saying," or "Close the book and don't read any more." Over the years, the spiritual fights that I have faced concerning this revelation have been extremely strong. I press on because God has shown me how important this is.

First, remember that the right hand is a metaphor for a ritual we do, and the forehead (frontlets/between our eyes) is a metaphor for, in remembrance of. Secondly, the devil mimics everything of God. If we can get a clear understanding of this, then we will recognize that the mark of the beast will be similar to God's mark. **So far, we have looked at two examples of things God told Israel to do (right hand) in remembrance of past occurrences (forehead).** Now we are going to take a look at one of God's marks that is going to blow this thing wide open.

Ex 13:6-10
6 **Seven days** thou shalt eat unleavened bread, and in the seventh day shall be **a feast** to the LORD.

7 **Unleavened bread** shall be eaten **seven days**; and there shall no leavened bread be seen with thee, neither shall there be leaven seen with thee in all thy quarters.

8 And thou shalt shew thy son in that day, saying, This is done because of that which the LORD did unto me when I came forth out of Egypt.

9 And **it shall be for a sign unto thee upon thine hand, and for a memorial between thine eyes,** that the LORD's law may be in thy mouth: for with a strong hand hath the LORD brought thee out of Egypt.

10 Thou shalt therefore **keep this ordinance in his season from year to year.**
KJV

The feast of unleavened bread was an annual seven-day feast that started with a day of holy convocation (no work), which today we would call a holiday because all work ceases. The last day was also a holiday where no work was done as in the first. This is an important Jewish holy day for believers because the first day starts after the Passover, which was foreshadowing the Lamb of God being slain to cover our past sins.

Think about this: It was seven days that started after the sacrifice of a lamb on Passover and ended with a feast. **It was required to be done every year.** It was a mark on their right hand and their forehead. It was a **memorial ritual** in **remembrance** of when God judged Egypt but passed over the children of Israel. This was God's mark on Israel, which pointed to the Messiah. Satan, who is the dragon of Revelation, is going to give power, a throne, and great authority to the beast whose mark will be taken by unbelievers.

Who is the Beast?

Now that we know what God's mark really means, let's dive deep into who the beast is before we expose his mark. I teach that we as believers are never to interpret the Bible when it comes to the metaphors and prophecy. We can't figure them out. I have seen on numerous occasions where people trying to figure out a hidden meaning in the scriptures, only to get lead astray by their own faulty assumptions. Self-interpretation will leave you **"Lost in the metaphor."** Peter confirms this understanding:

2 Peter 1:20-21
20 Knowing this first, that **no prophecy of the scripture is of any private interpretation.**
21 For the prophecy came not in old time by the will of man: but holy men of God spake as they were moved by the Holy Ghost.
KJV

     If the Holy Spirit gave the prophecy**, then the interpretation has to come from God.** We have to allow scripture to interpret scripture. If I want to know the meaning of the metaphor "beast," then I have to find the meaning in the scriptures and not come up with my own meaning. So where can we find the meaning for the metaphor of a beast?

Dan 7:2-3
2 Daniel spake and said, I saw in my vision by night, and, behold, the four winds of the heaven strove upon the great sea.
3 And **four great beasts came up from the sea,** diverse one from another.
KJV

     It is hard for me to resist wanting to share major parts of my previous books. Many of the points (keys of knowledge) I have already discussed (in-depth) in my earlier books shine a light on new discussions. If you want a deeper understanding of Biblical metaphors please read "Hidden In The Garden," or the excerpt "Hidden In The Metaphor." I cannot add all the information into this book because the space is limited. What I will share with you is that every single metaphor, parable, and dark saying utilized in the scriptures has the answer to its meaning in the scriptures. **Daniel and Proverbs are two books that shine the light on the most metaphors in the Bible.**

     Here we have Daniel having a vision where he sees four great beasts coming up out of the sea. The majority of the visions mentioned in scripture are allegorical in nature. Pay attention to what God is saying in the next scripture:

Num 12:6-8

6 And he said, Hear now my words: If there be a prophet among you, I the LORD will make myself known unto him **in a vision**, and will speak unto him in a dream.

7 My servant Moses is not so, who is faithful in all mine house.

8 With him will I speak mouth to mouth, even apparently, and **not in dark speeches**; and the similitude of the LORD shall he behold: wherefore then were ye not afraid to speak against my servant Moses?

KJV

God is stating that He speaks to Moses plainly, and not in dark speeches. Dark speeches are metaphors and stories with hidden meanings just like parables. The vision that Daniel is having is allegorical with a hidden meaning. The understanding is hidden in the metaphor. Again, the meanings of all metaphors in the scriptures are located in the scriptures. Some are easy to find (like many in Daniel); others you will never find without assistance from the Holy Spirit. Let's take a look at what is revealed by the unraveling of the metaphor of the four beasts in Daniel's vision. Back to the verses:

Dan 7:4-7

4 The **first was like a lion**, and had eagle's wings: I beheld till the wings thereof were plucked, and it was lifted up from the earth, and made stand upon the feet as a man, and a man's heart was given to it.

5 And behold another beast, **a second**, **like to a bear**, and it raised up itself on one side, and it had three ribs in the mouth of it between the teeth of it: and they said thus unto it, Arise, devour much flesh.

6 After this I beheld, and lo another, **like a leopard**, which had upon the back of it four wings of a fowl; the beast had also four heads; and dominion was given to it.

7 After this I saw in the night visions, and **behold a fourth beast, dreadful and terrible, and strong exceedingly; and it had great iron teeth: it devoured and brake in pieces, and stamped the residue with the feet of it: and it was diverse from all the beasts that were before it; and it had ten horns.**

KJV

We see that the four beasts, as described by Daniel, look like a lion, bear, leopard, and a dreadful unidentifiable creature. Notice that he did not have a simile to describe the fourth beast as an animal; just dreadful, terrible, and strong exceedingly. Now let's see what was revealed about these beasts. Please read these verses carefully because they will reveal other things, which are important to the understanding that comes later in the book.

Dan 7:15-17
15 I Daniel was grieved in my spirit in the midst of my body, and the visions of my head troubled me.
16 I came near unto one of them that stood by, and asked him the truth of all this. So he told me, and made me know the interpretation of the things.
17 **These great beasts, which are four, are four kings, which shall arise out of the earth.**
KJV

The scripture shows that Daniel was troubled in his spirit concerning the vision he had of the four beasts. He approached one of the angels that was near him and asked them for the interpretation of the vision. The angel tells Daniel that the four beasts are actually a metaphor for four kings (kingdoms). As you read down further you will see that each king represents the start of a new kingdom.

Then Daniel asks specifically about the fourth beast that was different from the others:

Dan 7:19-22
19 Then I would know the truth of **the fourth beast**, which was diverse from all the others, exceeding dreadful, whose teeth were of iron, and his nails of brass; which devoured, brake in pieces, and stamped the residue with his feet;
20 And of **the ten horns that were in his head**, and of the other **which came up, and before whom three fell**; even of that horn that had eyes, and a mouth that spake very great things, whose look was more stout than his fellows.
21 I beheld, and **the same horn made war with the saints, and prevailed against them**;

22 **Until the Ancient of days came**, and judgment was given to the saints of the most High; and the time came that the saints possessed the kingdom.
KJV

Let us look at some of the points that Daniel noted about the fourth beast. It is dreadful and different from the first three. It has ten horns on its head, and then one horn comes up and replaces three of the others. This same horn is at war with the saints and appears to be winning. The fourth beast will reign until Christ's return. Now back to Daniel and the revelation given by the angel.

Dan 7:23-28
23 Thus he said, The fourth beast shall be **the fourth kingdom** upon earth, which shall be diverse from all kingdoms, and shall devour the whole earth, and shall tread it down, and break it in pieces.
24 And the ten horns out of this kingdom are ten kings that shall arise: and another shall rise after them; and he shall be diverse from the first, and **he shall subdue three kings.**
25 And he shall speak great words against the most High, and shall wear out the saints of the most High, and think to change times and laws: and they shall be given into his hand until a time and times and the dividing of time.
26 But the judgment shall sit, and they shall take away his dominion, to consume and to destroy it unto the end.
27 And the kingdom and dominion, and the greatness of the kingdom under the whole heaven, shall be given to the people of the saints of the most High, whose kingdom is an everlasting kingdom, and all dominions shall serve and obey him.
28 Hitherto is the end of the matter. As for me Daniel, my cogitations much troubled me, and my countenance changed in me: but I kept the matter in my heart.
KJV

Rev 13:1-10
13:1 And I stood upon the sand of the sea, and saw **a beast rise up out of the sea,** having **seven heads and ten horns**, and upon his horns **ten crowns**, and upon his heads the name of blasphemy.
2 And **the beast which I saw was like unto a leopard, and his feet were as the feet of a bear, and his mouth as the mouth of a**

lion: and the dragon gave him his power, and his seat, and great authority.

3 And I saw one of his heads as it were wounded to death; and his deadly wound was healed: and all the world wondered after the beast.

4 And they worshipped the dragon which gave power unto the beast: and they worshipped the beast, saying, Who is like unto the beast? who is able to make war with him?

5 And there was given unto him **a mouth** speaking great things and blasphemies; and power was given unto him to continue **forty and two months.**

6 And he opened his mouth in blasphemy against God, to blaspheme his name, and his tabernacle, and them that dwell in heaven.

7 And it was given unto him to make war with the saints, and to overcome them: and power was given him over all kindreds, and tongues, and nations.

8 And all that dwell upon the earth shall worship him, whose names are not written in the book of life of the Lamb slain from the foundation of the world.

9 If any man have an ear, let him hear.

10 **He that leadeth into captivity shall go into captivity**: he that **killeth with the sword must be killed with the sword.** Here is the patience and the faith of the saints.
KJV

The words spoken to Daniel by the angel reveals to us that the beast is a kingdom or nation. We also realize that Daniel and John were both speaking about the same beast. When we compare the description of the last (fourth) beast of Daniel and the beast of Revelation, we realize that Daniel's fourth beast is the beast of Revelation that gives the mark.

John (Rev) and Daniel are standing on the sand of a seashore looking into the sea. They see a beast coming up out of the sea. Remember, we **must** always look for an understanding of metaphors, in the scriptures. What do the scriptures tell us about the sea?

Isa 17:12

12 Woe to the multitude of many people, **which make a noise like the noise of the seas**; and to the rushing of nations, that make a rushing like the rushing of mighty waters! KJV

We find in Isaiah 17:12 that the prophet uses a simile to compare a multitude of people to the sea. The sea that Daniel and John saw the beast coming up out of is a metaphor for a multitude of people. Now let's take a look at a scripture, which will confirm what I am saying, and give us a clearer picture:

Rev 17:15
15 And he saith unto me, **The waters** which thou sawest, where the whore sitteth, are **peoples, and multitudes**, and nations, and tongues.
KJV

The meaning of what Daniel and John saw is a multitude of people forming a kingdom; this is the meaning of the beast coming up out of the sea. This confirms again that the beast in Rev 13 is a metaphor for a nation or group of nations.

We spoke earlier about Daniel identifying the three beasts as animals and the angel revealed that they were three kingdoms. Most scholars including myself identify the first three as the Babylonian Empire, Mede Persian Empire, and Grecian Empire and scripture confirms this. The Roman Empire took the place of the Grecians, as this was the ruling world empire during the time John wrote Revelation. This is the fourth beast in Daniel's vision of the beasts coming up out of the sea, and all these beasts coincide with another vision of Daniel's.

Dan 2:36-44
36 This is the dream; and we will tell the interpretation thereof before the king.
37 Thou, O king, art a king of kings: for the God of heaven hath given thee a kingdom, power, and strength, and glory.
38 And wheresoever the children of men dwell, the beasts of the field and the fowls of the heaven hath he given into thine hand, and hath made thee ruler over them all. Thou art this head of gold.
39 And **after thee shall arise another kingdom inferior to thee, and another third kingdom of brass, which shall bear rule over all the earth.**

40 And **the fourth kingdom** shall be strong as iron: forasmuch as iron breaketh in pieces and subdueth all things: and as iron that breaketh all these, shall it break in pieces and bruise.

41 And whereas thou sawest the feet and toes, part of potters' clay, and part of iron, the kingdom shall be divided; but there shall be in it of the strength of the iron, forasmuch as thou sawest the iron mixed with miry clay.

42 And as the toes of the feet were part of iron, and part of clay, so the kingdom shall be partly strong, and partly broken.

43 And whereas thou sawest iron mixed with miry clay, they shall mingle themselves with the seed of men: but they shall not cleave one to another, even as iron is not mixed with clay.

44 And in the days of these kings shall the God of heaven set up a kingdom, which shall never be destroyed: and the kingdom shall not be left to other people, but it shall break in pieces and consume all these kingdoms, and it shall stand for ever.

KJV

Daniel is asked by King Nebuchadnezzar to give an interpretation of a dream that the king does not remember. Daniel tells the king that true interpretation comes from God and if he gives him some time, he will go to God and come back with the interpretation. Daniel receives the dream and interpretation from God. He is shown a giant statue with a gold head, silver upper torso, brass for a midsection, legs of iron with feet of iron and clay mixed together.

Daniel is speaking to the King of Babylon, and he identifies Babylon as the first kingdom (first beast), represented by the gold head of the statue. He then describes the upper torso of the statue as a lesser kingdom of the Medes and Persians (second beast). The midsection of brass represents the next kingdom that replaced the Medes and the Persians as world rulers, which is the Grecian Empire (third beast). The final kingdom can be no other than the Romans (fourth beast and beast of Revelation) who supplanted the Greeks as world rulers. The Roman name comes from their first king Romulus who was one of two twin brothers raised by wolves. This could be foreshadowing to the beastly nature of the kingdom (more on this later in the book). This kingdom was ruling Judea (Israel) during the time of Christ when John wrote Revelation. The Roman Empire seemed to be on the verge of collapse during the third century ce (common era) but was brought back from the brink, transformed into Europe and then what we know today as the European Union. Now that we know Rome is the beast. What is the mark of Rome?

We understand that the mark is something you do in remembrance of an event. This is not hard to grasp, it is just difficult to accept when all your life you have been told it was a microchip that would be placed in our hand or forehead. The misconception about the microchip is fortified by a wrong understanding of Rev 13: 17. This is the scripture they use to support the microchip:

Rev 13:17-18
17 And that **no man might buy or sell, save he that had the mark,** or the name of the beast, or the number of his name.
18 Here is wisdom. Let him that hath understanding count the number of the beast: for it is the number of a man; and his number is **Six hundred threescore and six.**
KJV

When people today read that you won't be able to buy or sell without the mark of the beast, they see a computer chip that needs to be scanned as the perfect fit. The problem is the scripture says "mark, name, or the number." You need to have one of the three it would seem but the truth is you need all three. What many don't realize is the Greek word "e" pronounced (ay) and translated "or" can also read "and", "than", "that", "but", and so on. The translator used the word "or" because it made the most sense to him. In the same way, he says it is a mark on the right hand OR the forehead. Scripture from the Old Testament reveals it should have been translated right hand "and" forehead just as God's mark on Israel.

I am going to give you one of the biggest shocks of your life. The scripture in the Greek actually could also read that you will not be able to buy or sell save he that have the mark, name of the beast, and the number of his name. You would need all three. Why? All three are on the money that you use to buy and sell. Now take out a dollar bill and get your scuba gear 'cause we are going deeper.

Chapter 8

Almighty Dollar

Rev 13:17-18
**17 And that no man might buy or sell, save he that had the
mark, or the name of the beast, or the number of his name.
18 Here is wisdom. Let him that hath understanding count the
number of the beast: for it is the number of a man; and his
number is Six hundred threescore and six.**
KJV

The reason you can't buy or sell without the mark, name, and number is because it is on the money. Now, I am in no way endorsing anyone, especially a Christian, to go out and allow someone to put a computer chip in your hand, much less your forehead. If God commands that His people should not get tattoos, then it would be obvious that we should not be putting chips in our bodies. Nothing good can come from implanting things that can be used to monitor and track us in this evil age.

The question is already answered that a chip is not the mark of the beast; yet, it has been cleverly used to hide the identity of what the mark really is. We utilize chips in credit cards. Many have said chips would replace the dollar but that will never happen. You can't hack a dollar bill, but any chip can be hacked sooner or later. The average person does not realize that the dollar is the standard of commerce used around the world. All international trade is done by the dollar standard. Many have tried to get this changed to a gold standard so all trade would be linked to gold. Most of those who have tried (like Khadafy and Saddam Hussein) have come up missing.

Selling of souls

I want to share a revelation with you before we get into how the dollar contains the name, number, and the mark of the beast. Sadly, many of today's Christians have strayed from believing the Word of God. They have become entwined in a worldly belief system. When spiritual minded Christians try to explain to them the diabolical things happening in the world, under the cover of good, they believe it is some type of conspiracy theory. When you show them that these things are written in the Word of God, some will still believe the kingdom of Satan's denials of the wickedness over God's truth. Here is an example of what they find unbelievable: The souls of people are being bought and sold on a daily basis.

The whole world has already received the mark in some form or fashion. They do things in remembrance of their ancestors. They even believe they can be guided by and talk to their ancestors even though God has said that necromancy (talking to the dead) is an abomination. They have sold themselves and their children to demonic spirits. They have spirit parties (mark on the hand) in remembrance (mark on the forehead) of when they sold themselves (or were sold by parents) to these spirits. We have entertainers who have made covenants with demons and fallen angels. They are selling their own souls for money, fame, and power.

They call the demons who they have sold themselves to their spirit guides, angels, or their alternative persona. When singers talk about their alter egos, they are talking about fallen angels and demons. In interviews, many mention their alter egos taking over their bodies. The very term "alter ego" was coined by Cicero, a first century bce **Roman** politician (not surprising). The term means the other self. This self is an unclean spirit/s living in the flesh. They confirm this truth with their very songs and then subliminally introduce their fans to the same evil forces through the music (see book "**Assault on Innocence**").

I have a lot of experience teaching teenagers and young adults in South Florida. Three of the main pagan religions in the area are Santeria (Cuban voodoo), Obeah (Jamaican voodoo), and Hu (Haitian voodoo). Many other countries have these forms of voodoo also. I have literally taught classes where these young people share testimonies of themselves or their family members being sold to demons. These practices are kept secret from the public, and most adults will never admit to being a part of this. It is also amusing that those on the outside looking in will tell you it is no different from any other religion. Yet, when you talk to those involved or those who came out of these beliefs, they will tell you straightforward that these spirits are demons and fallen angels. The Bible testifies to this fact:

Ps 106:37
37 Yea, they sacrificed their sons and their daughters **unto devils**, KJV

The young people are more ready to expose the truth once they know you know about it and can help them get delivered from these demons. They have not bought into the religion because it was forced upon them by their parents. As they learn who and what these things really are, they seek to be free from these controlling spirits. These demons and fallen angels have a destiny that cannot be changed, and all those in league with them will share the same fate. If your spirit guide, who you sold yourself to, is headed to hell know that his ticket says, "Seating for two."

I have had many tell me that they have to throw a birthday party every year for the spirit that owns them under threat of penalty. This is something that is well known in the Cuban communities that practice Santeria. These spirits make their lives a living hell if they don't serve them. People, this stuff is real!

In ancient times, they would sacrifice their kids to the demons but today they also sell their kids to them to acquire wealth, fame, and status. They are dooming themselves and their children if they don't find Christ. Scripture confirms that these things would be happening. In end time prophecy, God gives us a visual of what would happen right before the return of Christ Jesus. Please read the next scripture carefully, which describes the destruction of a city and the merchandise sold in it. This city is symbolically called Babylon:

Rev 18:10-13

10 Standing afar off for the fear of her torment, saying, Alas, alas, **that great city Babylon, that mighty city! For in one hour is thy judgment come.**

11 And the merchants of the earth shall weep and mourn over her; for no man buyeth their merchandise any more:

12 The merchandise of gold, and silver, and precious stones, and of pearls, and fine linen, and purple, and silk, and scarlet, and all thyine wood, and all manner vessels of ivory, and all manner vessels of most precious wood, and of brass, and iron, and marble,

13 And cinnamon, and odours, and ointments, and frankincense, and wine, and oil, and fine flour, and wheat, and beasts, and sheep, and horses, and chariots, and slaves, **and souls of men**.

KJV

Please notice that slaves are mentioned before souls, so this is not about people sold as slaves, these are the souls of people being bought and sold.

I want you to also understand that others are signing contracts in the spirit realm and are oblivious to it. **When you accept a tradition and do a ritual in remembrance of an event in honor of Satan's kingdom, you are pledging allegiance to the forces of evil, even if you do not realize it.** Satan has no problem in capturing those entering his territory through the lack of knowledge. This same lack of knowledge allows Christians to practice satanic rituals called traditions, celebrations, and holidays. They unwittingly reject the knowledge of God and embrace Satan.

Hos 4:6

6 My **people are destroyed for lack of knowledge**: because thou hast rejected knowledge, I will also reject thee, that thou shalt be no priest to me: seeing thou hast forgotten the law of thy God, **I will also forget thy children.**

KJV

Any ritual done in honor of demons and devils is a mark on our right hand and forehead. As was revealed earlier, when you send your kids out to Halloween do you realize that it is a ritual done (right hand) in remembrance of (forehead) the dead and the forces of evil? Is a person in the deep jungles of Africa going to get a computer chip? No! Yet, they are doing rituals (right hand) in remembrance of (forehead) pagan gods, traditions, and holidays just like the rest of the world. Now do you see how the whole world is caught up in this? The world has already received the mark.

Rev 12:9
9 And the great dragon was cast out, that old serpent, called the Devil, and Satan, **which deceiveth the whole world**: he was cast out into the earth, and his angels were cast out with him.
KJV

I know many people who are reading this book will realize they are caught up in the mark. The answer to this realization is to make the correction by refusing to partake in these things. The contract used to sell stolen goods is illegitimate. The devil does not want people who have sold themselves to know this. Satan and his kingdom have only one purpose, to lead people to death and hell.

John 10:10-11
10 The thief cometh not, but for to steal, and to kill, and to destroy: I am come that they might have life, and that they might have it more abundantly.
11 I am the good shepherd: the good shepherd giveth his life for the sheep.
KJV

Christ came with the Fathers purpose to redeem us from death. **The contract can be voided according to the Word of God. All you have to do is petition God to take back possession of the stolen goods because the truth be told, we all belong to Him.**

Ezek 18:4
4 Behold, **all souls are mine**; as the soul of the father, so also the soul of the son is mine: the soul that sinneth, it shall die.
KJV

For those who have sold themselves, only God can free a soul that has been sold to the devil. Only the true owner can recover stolen goods.

Ezek 18:21-23
21 But if the wicked will turn from all his sins that he hath committed, and keep all my statutes, and do that which is lawful and right, he shall surely live, he shall not die.
22 All his transgressions that he hath committed, they shall not be mentioned unto him: in his righteousness that he hath done he shall live.
23 **Have I any pleasure at all that the wicked should die? saith the Lord GOD: and not that he should return from his ways, and live?** (KJV)

Those of us (Christians) who realize we have participated in things that caused us to receive the mark, even as we claim to be servants of God, must go to the mercy seat in prayer and repent. Renounce all the activities of the enemy to include traditions, rituals, and religious holidays not of God. God is merciful.

The wrong thing to do is to allow the devil to get you to reject the credible truth you are receiving, so you can continue walking in the way of the world. The enemy will fight you in your mind to find a way to justify that what you are feeling in your heart is wrong. Do not allow him to bury the truth. Remember, eternity is a long time to be wrong. We're not done yet, put in your mouthpiece and breath, we are going deeper.

The dollar

Please grab that dollar bill. I am going to show you some of the things hidden on it that will reveal that it is **not** dedicated to the God you and I trust in. The dollar is what Revelation is speaking of when it says you will not be able to buy or sell without the mark, name, or number.

Rev 13:17
17 And that no man might buy or sell, save he that had **the mark**, or **the name of the beast**, or **the number of his name.** KJV

There is so much that we can discuss concerning the dollar bill. The God Moloch is on it in the form of an owl. The Masons (Illuminati) have their name and symbols all over it. There is a skull and a voodoo priest on it. It goes on and on and on. We don't have space for a 1000 page book. We are going to concentrate on three things, the name of the beast, the mark of the beast, and the number of his name. (See, this book's Facebook page for other symbols.)

What does this all mean? It means that the beast (first beast) of Revelation 13 is the Roman Empire. **The name** of the beast is **Rome or Roman** in some form. **The number** of the name is **Roman numeral**. The number of the beast is 666. **The mark** of the beast, which is something we do in remembrance of an event, is going to come from the Roman Empire. The mark is tied to the number.

Something the Roman Empire did in remembrance of an event is the mark of the beast. The saturnalia and winter solstice festival was to the Romans what Passover and the feast of unleavened bread are to Israel. If Passover and the feast of unleavened bread was the mark of Israel, then the saturnalia was the mark of the Roman Empire. It is the mark of the beast, a seven-day feast leading up to the winter solstice and the birth of the sun god. In Greco-Roman culture, Apollo was worshiped as the sun god. In the latter part of the Roman Empire, this distinction went to Sol Invictus. This is parallel to Tammuz the sun/fertility god of Canaan. It was an annual celebration done in remembrance of the birth of the new sun. It was a mark on their right hand and their forehead.

Rev 13:17-18
17 And that no man might buy or sell, save he that had **the mark, or the name of the beast, or the number of his name.**
18 Here is wisdom. Let him that hath understanding count **the number of the beast: for it is the number of a man; and his number is Six hundred threescore and six.**
KJV

If what I am saying lines up with scripture, then the Roman name, number of the name (Rome), and the mark must be on the dollar bill in some form or fashion. We have to understand that if the Devil is working in deception, the mark, name, and number will not be plainly written out but will appear in some form of disguise on the dollar.

I want to take you to the great seal on the back of the dollar bill. The seal (front and back) is contained in the two circles, one with the picture of a pyramid and the other of an eagle. I could make it simple by saying you can spell out Rome using the letters but it is deeper than that. Please take note of the words directly over the eye encased in the triangle (top pyramid). The Latin (Roman's language) words read ANNUIT COEPTIS but what do they mean, and where do they come from?

From the Online Eptymology Dictionary:

Annuit Coeptis

Latin Juppiter omnipotes, audacibus annue coeptis "All-powerful Jupiter favor (my) daring undertakings," line 625 of book IX of Virgil's "Aeneid."

The term comes from the epic poem by Virgil the "Aeneid" written around 25 bce. The story of the founding of Rome is told in the form of an epic poem. The hero of the story Aeneas is asking the false god Jupiter (Rome's head god) to grant favor in his attempt to conquer the land (Juppiter omnipotes, audacibus annue coeptis). These words are taken from the story of the founding of Rome, the beast of Revelation. Yes, the Latin statement that literally commences the foundation of the beast is on the dollar bill.

In addition, why is a pyramid on the US dollar? My initial thought on studying the pyramid is that it must have some link with Egypt but upon reconsideration, it again points to the beast of Rome. During the writing of Revelation, Egypt was already part of the Roman Empire. Egypt was a territory of the beast up to 400 ce. When we look at the pyramid on the seal, we again see Rome. Rome is on the money and this explains why the Roman numerals are at the base of the pyramid. Why are all these Roman (Latin) words and images on the American dollar? Don't just read the last sentence, think about it. WHAT DO ALL THESE ROMAN BASED WORDS AND SYMBOLS HAVE TO DO WITH AMERICA? America is a nation formed out of Europe. Spain, France, and England had possession of this land stolen from Native Americans. American settlers rose up and took America from those three nations who were themselves taking it from the natives. Remember that in the Bible "Horn" is a symbol for a nation.

Dan 7:8
8 I considered the horns, and, behold, **there came up among them another little horn, before whom there were three of the first horns plucked up by the roots:** and, behold, in this horn were **eyes like the eyes of man**, and **a mouth speaking great things**.
KJV

The founding fathers were the children of Europe who conquered what we call America. England, France, and Spain were all uprooted and the United States of America took their place. The question is, what model of government is our country founded on?

There is more. It should also be noted that the symbol for the Roman Empire military (legion) was the golden eagle called Aquila. Take a look at the image on the next page. Does it look familiar?

The letters SPQR is an initialism of a Latin phrase Senatus Populusque Romanus (the people and senate of Rome). Even though SPQR is not on the dollar, it is important to remember because when the image of the beast is explained this will become very relevant.

Before we go any further, stop here and ask yourself if you really want to know the truth. This truth is heavy and is going to be hard to swallow for many. The evidence is compelling and it is going to shatter the foundation of many false beliefs, which can be hard for some to accept. For those who answered "yes," let's dive a little deeper.

The Number

Diabolical, yes, that's the word, it is diabolical how they placed the 666 on the dollar. I want you to take a dollar bill and examine it closely to see if you can find it. Search as diligently as you can. I will wait right here until you have exhausted your search.

Stop playing! Go search that dollar.

Ok, couldn't find it could you? Now I am sure somewhere in the world, there is a dollar bill with the numbers 666 in the serial number but that is not it. The way they hid the numbers on the dollar I must admit is very creative. It is right under your nose, and the funny thing is most peoples noses are formed somewhat like a pyramid. Yes, it is hidden in the numbers under the pyramid.

Located under the pyramid on the dollar are the **Roman** numerals MDCCLXXVI that equals the number 1776. I will often ask groups to take the numbers and form them into two pyramids. Take a couple seconds, look at the numbers (1776), and see if you can do it. Think hard; just don't skip down to the answer. Things that are hard mentally increase the capacity of understanding by exercising the mind.

There is a good chance that you came up with flipping a seven with the other seven as a solution. This answer is what people normally come up with but that is not it. The answer is coded. You have to take the numbers and break them down to form two pyramids. The numbers will actually form the two pyramids above them on the dollar. The first group of numbers taken out of 1776 will form the bottom pyramid with the flat top, and the numbers left over will form the pointed triangle on top with the eye inside. The second group of numbers will not only form the shape of the second pyramid but will also identify whose eye is in it. There is only one way to do this. You are going to need a piece of paper and a pencil. We are going to subtract two groups of numbers from 1776 to form two pyramids. I want you to write 1000, then write 100 on top of it, then 10 on top of that. Center the numbers. It will look like this:

10
100
1000

Do you see the pyramid with the stairs going up on the side? It represents the bottom pyramid on the seal. Now subtract the numbers 1110 from the 1776. What number are you left with? Take the number that is left, and form the top pyramid. Take 600 and place 60 on top and lastly the 6 on top of that.

6
60
600

This is not a coincidence; the numbers identify the owner of the eye inside the top pyramid (triangle). There have been many names to identify the eye on the dollar. It is called the eye of Lucifer, eye of Horus, eye of providence and many other names (Eye of Odin as will be shown later). Yet the number identifies what the eye is and whom it belongs to. The Bible says it is the number of a man.

So now, we have the hidden name revealed on the dollar. We also have the hidden number revealed on the dollar. Therefore, we are left with the question of where the mark is on the dollar. Remember that the mark on your right hand is something that you do in remembrance of something, which is the mark on your forehead. So how is this hidden on the dollar? Very cleverly. Get the keys to that time machine, we are about to take another trip.

We are back to the past; yes, we have touched down back in Jerusalem the day that God took Ezekiel into visions showing him what was happening at the temple. Remember what we learned earlier. The women weep for Tammuz through the night. The women stop crying just before the winter solstice (at the break of day) when the new sun rises. They stop weeping as the sun appears and they bring out a young boy representing the sun god. The men, who were at the east of the temple watching the sunrise, and worshiping it, were celebrating the birth of the sun god. Ezekiel was taken into the vision the day before and shown the whole worship ritual that lead into the next day. So what was the day that the vision started?

Ezek 8:1
8:1 And it came to pass in the **sixth year**, in the **sixth month**, in the **fifth day** of the month, as I sat in mine house, and the elders of

Judah sat before me, that the hand of the Lord GOD fell there upon me.
KJV

If Ezekiel is shown the vision on the 6th year 6th month and 5th day, then the winter solstice (the next day) falls on the 6th year, 6th month, and 6th day. The number of the man is the birthday of the man worshipped as the sun god. Tammuz is the man. In Egypt, he is called Horus (reincarnated Osiris), the one-eyed sun god. Both gods are representations of the first demon-possessed man worshiped as a god named Nimrod. We will see later how he is even linked to Santa Claus through another false god that is worshipped. All of their birthdays are on the winter solstice the holy day of the Roman Empire called the Saturnalia when they give honor to their gods through the same rituals that we utilize today for Christmas. The number is not the mark; the day of celebration that it identifies is the mark. We deceive ourselves thinking we are honoring Christ. Christ's very own words testify of the world's and many Christians' deception:

Mark 7:6-7
6 He answered and said unto them, Well hath Esaias prophesied of you hypocrites, as it is written, This people honoureth me with their lips, but their heart is far from me.
7 Howbeit **in vain do they worship me, teaching for doctrines the commandments of men.**
KJV

We now see that through deception and craftiness that the name, number, and mark of the beast are all on the dollar bill. It is impossible to buy or sell in this present world without it.

Now I don't want you to get nervous and think you have to give away all your money and stop buying and selling. God did not say that to use the money is to take the mark. He just said we would not be able to buy or sell without the name, number, and mark of the beast. We are not worshiping when we utilize money to buy goods. I do not want the devil to put in your mind that I am saying it is wrong to use the money. Remember Christ's wisdom:

Matt 22:17-21
17 Tell us therefore, What thinkest thou? **Is it lawful to give tribute unto Caesar, or not?**
18 But Jesus perceived their wickedness, and said, Why tempt ye me, ye hypocrites?
19 Shew me the tribute money. And they brought unto him a penny.
20 And he saith unto them, **Whose is this image and superscription?**
21 They say unto him, Caesar's. Then saith he unto them, **Render therefore unto Caesar the things which are Caesar's; and unto God the things that are God's.**
KJV

It is Caesar's money so we give to him what is his, but all our worship is to go to God and no other. We also cannot allow the enemy to deceive us into giving him worship instead of God. What did God tell us not to do? What are we to overcome? I am not here to scare you. I am here to warn and teach you. I know some people who read this are going to have what seems like every fiber of their flesh fighting to reject the teaching of the book. Flesh does not want to give up Christmas. I want you to read the scripture below very carefully. Say a short prayer and ask God to guide you in the truth and then read it again:

Rev 14:9-11
9 And the third angel followed them, saying with a loud voice, **If any man worship the beast and his image, and receive his mark in his forehead, or in his hand,**
10 The same shall drink of the wine of the wrath of God, which is poured out without mixture into the cup of his indignation; and he shall be tormented with fire and brimstone in the presence of the holy angels, and in the presence of the Lamb:
11 And the smoke of their torment ascendeth up for ever and ever: and they have no rest day nor night, who worship the beast and his image, and whosoever receiveth the mark of his name.
KJV

Rev 19:20
20 And the beast was taken, and with him **the false prophet that wrought miracles before him, with which he deceived them that**

had received the mark of the beast, and them that worshipped his image. These both were cast alive into a lake of fire burning with brimstone.
KJV

Taking the mark and worshiping the beast's image is what causes this judgment to fall on the people. Did you notice, it is the **false prophet** that is with the beast of Rome? Through him, the deception of the mark and image is put forth. Who do you think is the false prophet of Rome? Let's reiterate a point from the front of the book of how Christmas was syncretized into Christianity:

According to a Roman almanac, the Christian festival of Christmas was celebrated in Rome by ad 336. **Note the name Christmas (Christ-Mass). The word mass is a term used in the Roman Catholic CHURCH, not in the Bible.**

I am going to let you meditate on what you just read. Please take a break. When you come back, we are going to crank up the time machine once again. It is time to expose the image of the beast.

Chapter 9

Image of the Beast

We arrive around 575 bce. We are in a wooded area outside of the city of Babylon. Directly in front of us, we see a naked man groveling in the grass and dirt as if he is a wild animal. His hairs are long and ragged and his fingernails look more like claws. He is eating grass like a cow, and his appearance is more like that of a beast than a man. You stare perplexed, not understanding what this has to do with what I have been teaching you. The man we are observing is Nebuchadnezzar, king of the Babylonian Empire.

I know you are wondering what happened to him. Let's investigate. Seven years prior, while Nebuchadnezzar was sleeping in his palace, he had a dream:

Dan 4:13-16
13 I saw in the visions of my head upon my bed, and, behold, a watcher and an holy one came down from heaven;
14 He cried aloud, and said thus, **Hew down the tree**, and cut off his branches, shake off his leaves, and scatter his fruit: let the beasts get away from under it, and the fowls from his branches:
15 Nevertheless leave the stump of his roots in the earth, even with a band of iron and brass, in the tender grass of the field; and let it be wet with the dew of heaven, and let his portion be with the beasts in the grass of the earth:
16 **Let his heart be changed from man's, and let a beast's heart be given unto him; and let seven times pass over him.**
KJV

Those who have read "Hidden In The Garden" are smiling right now. You actually understand much of the scripture. You are not lost in the metaphor. Give yourself a hand.

The vision was a prophecy from God in the form of a dark saying (riddle). Nebuchadnezzar is the tree that is about to be cut down. He did not understand the dream, so he called for the wise men of the kingdom, who could not give the interpretation. He then asked Daniel, whom he called by his Babylonian name Belteshazzar.

Dan 4:18
18 This dream I king Nebuchadnezzar have seen. Now thou, O Belteshazzar, declare the interpretation thereof, forasmuch as all the wise men of my kingdom are not able to make known unto me the interpretation: but thou art able; for the spirit of the holy gods is in thee.
KJV

It is important for you to read the story because there is a great revelation in it of how God humbled Nebuchadnezzar. Please read the verses carefully and see if it reminds you of anything that you have already read in the book.

Dan 4:19-26
19 Then Daniel, whose name was Belteshazzar, was astonied for one hour, and his thoughts troubled him. The king spake, and said, Belteshazzar, let not the dream, or the interpretation thereof, trouble thee. Belteshazzar answered and said, My lord, the dream be to them that hate thee, and the interpretation thereof to thine enemies.
20 The tree that thou sawest, which grew, and was strong, whose height reached unto the heaven, and the sight thereof to all the earth;
21 Whose leaves were fair, and the fruit thereof much, and in it was meat for all; under which the beasts of the field dwelt, and upon whose branches the fowls of the heaven had their habitation:
22 It is thou, O king, that art grown and become strong: for thy greatness is grown, and reacheth unto heaven, and thy dominion to the end of the earth.
23 And whereas the king saw a watcher and an holy one coming down from heaven, and saying, Hew the tree down, and destroy it; yet leave the stump of the roots thereof in the earth, even with a

band of iron and brass, in the tender grass of the field; and let it be wet with the dew of heaven, and let his portion be with the beasts of the field, till seven times pass over him;

24 This is the interpretation, O king, and this is the decree of the most High, which is come upon my lord the king:

25 That they shall drive thee from men, and thy dwelling shall be with the beasts of the field, and they shall make thee to eat grass as oxen, and they shall wet thee with the dew of heaven, and seven times shall pass over thee, till thou know that the most High ruleth in the kingdom of men, and giveth it to whomsoever he will.

26 And whereas they commanded to leave the stump of the tree roots; thy kingdom shall be sure unto thee, after that thou shalt have known that the heavens do rule

KJV

I teach my Biblical students how important it is to guard what they say out of their mouth. The Bible contains a powerful revelation of how Cain opened the door of his mouth and let murder in (see "Assault On Innocence" book). Christ also comes to the door and knocks and by our confession, we open the door (mouth) and start the process of salvation in our heart. We sign contracts with the enemy also by the very words of our mouth. These words can justify or condemn us, so we need to be careful of what we speak. Sadly, Nebuchadnezzar found this out the hard way. I know these scriptures are long but it is important that you read them to get the deep revelations that God has placed in them.

Dan 4:29-37

29 At the end of twelve months he walked in the palace of the kingdom of Babylon.

30 **The king spake, and said, Is not this great Babylon, that I have built for the house of the kingdom by the might of my power, and for the honour of my majesty?**

31 While the word was in the king's mouth, there fell a voice from heaven, saying, O king Nebuchadnezzar, to thee it is spoken; The kingdom is departed from thee.

32 And they shall drive thee from men, and thy dwelling shall be with the beasts of the field: they shall make thee to eat grass as oxen, and seven times shall pass over thee, until thou know that the most High ruleth in the kingdom of men, and giveth it to whomsoever he will.

33 The same hour was the thing fulfilled upon Nebuchadnezzar: and he was driven from men, and did eat grass as oxen, and his body was wet with the dew of heaven, till his hairs were grown like eagles' feathers, and his nails like birds' claws.

34 And at the end of the days **I Nebuchadnezzar lifted up mine eyes unto heaven, and mine understanding returned unto me, and I blessed the most High**, and I praised and honoured him that liveth for ever, whose dominion is an everlasting dominion, and his kingdom is from generation to generation:

35 And all the inhabitants of the earth are reputed as nothing: and he doeth according to his will in the army of heaven, and among the inhabitants of the earth: and none can stay his hand, or say unto him, What doest thou?

36 At the same time my reason returned unto me; and for the glory of my kingdom, mine honour and brightness returned unto me; and my counsellors and my lords sought unto me; and I was established in my kingdom, and excellent majesty was added unto me.

37 Now **I Nebuchadnezzar praise and extol and honour the King of heaven, all whose works are truth, and his ways judgment: and those that walk in pride he is able to abase.**
KJV

God is the one that established Nebuchadnezzar to fulfill His purpose in the earth. When Nebuchadnezzar opened his mouth to praise himself, and not God, for the greatness of his kingdom, the prophecy went into effect. God humbled him by reducing him to a beast. Yet even in that God showed mercy and held his kingdom for him until the time appointed (seven years) passed. The judgment was fulfilled. Nebuchadnezzar realized it was not about him it was about God. He realized that God was in control. God was the true ruler in heaven and on earth. This is when he no longer walked as a beast but as a man.

Now let me show you how no one teaches like God. Do you remember the four beasts that Daniel saw come out of the sea? Do you remember the first beast that was a lion with wings? What happened to it? If you pay attention to what happens to the first beast it will not only confirm it is Babylon but also give insight into the image of the beast. Who teaches like God?

Dan 7:4
4 The first was like a lion, and had eagle's wings: I beheld till the wings thereof were plucked, and **it was lifted up from the earth,** and **made stand upon the feet as a man, and a man's heart was given to it.**
KJV

Are you starting to understand why we had to take a trip back to Nebuchadnezzar to understand what the image of the beast is? I am taking this slow because it is extremely important for your Christian walk that you understand this. When we as men walk in self-will, pride, or honoring self, the Bible says we are foolish and brutish. We become just like the fool (according to scripture) that does not believe in God because even though we say we believe, we refuse to honor Him by giving Him His rightful place in our lives. We become brutish, walking in our own honor just like Nebuchadnezzar. We become beasts. We put on the image of the beast.

Ps 49:12-20
12 Nevertheless man, though in honor, does not remain; **He is like the beasts that perish.**
13 This is the way of those who are foolish, And of their posterity who approve their sayings. Selah
14 Like sheep they are laid in the grave; Death shall feed on them; The upright shall have dominion over them in the morning; And their beauty shall be consumed in the grave, far from their dwelling.
15 But God will redeem my soul from the power of the grave, For He shall receive me. Selah
16 Do not be afraid when one becomes rich, When the glory of his house is increased;
17 For when he dies he shall carry nothing away; His glory shall not descend after him.
18 Though while he lives he blesses himself (For men will praise you when you do well for yourself),
19 He shall go to the generation of his fathers; They shall never see light.
20 A man who is in honor, **yet does not understand, Is like the beasts that perish.**
NKJV

Daniel saw all four beasts come out of the ocean and they all represent nations of men. Only one of the beasts stands up and receives the heart of a man, only one. If you do Biblical research on Nebuchadnezzar, you will find that the king walked in righteousness, upright before God for the rest of his days. **When you are weak before God, you are strong. When you humble yourself, God will exalt you.** All four kingdoms started out as beasts but the only one that stood up as a man and was given the heart of a man was the one whose king was humbled and realized God is the one who rules and not man.

All the rest of the beasts stayed in the same state from the beginning to the end. The other kingdoms, want to rule themselves or be ruled by a king, and not by God.

The image of the beast is self-rule

Many years ago, God showed me that when we walk in the carnal mindset, in the flesh, we walk as beasts. Beasts walk on all fours and this is not what God intended for humankind. God made man to walk upright with our heads being the highest part of our bodies. Beasts walk with their heads down on all fours with their bodies (flesh) level to their heads. The head, heart, and flesh being on the same level is symbolic. **When we walk upright, it symbolizes that we are allowing our head to rule. Our head is on top at the highest point. We submit to God through Christ who is our true head.**

Think about it, there is no other mammal (beast) that walks continually upright on two legs. Some like monkeys and kangaroos do it for very short periods, but their norm is to walk on all fours. God made man to walk in an upright position, showing that we are His creation and have a purpose beyond other created beasts. We are created with a spirit, soul, and body. All other beasts have souls, bodies, and the breath of life but they are not spiritually linked to God. Our spirit is the part of us given by God that links us to Him and the spirit realm. Adam was created as more than a beast of the field. After Adam fell, man still walked on two legs as God created us; however, we remained in a fallen state because our spirit was inoperable due to Adam's sin. This is why God told Adam that the day he eats from the tree of the knowledge of good and evil (The tree is Satan, see "Hidden In The Garden") he would surely die. Adam died spiritually. He was still walking on two feet, but spiritually he was on all fours walking like a beast controlled by the flesh and his carnal desires. Humanity took on the image of the beast.

Sidenote: Do you realize that the fallen angels received the same fate when they were cast out of heaven? The metaphor of the serpent going on his belly is the fallen angels controlled by fleshly desires like men. If you want a deeper understanding of this, please read "Hidden In The Garden."

Christ did not come to save spirits. He came to save souls. Our soul needs to be transformed through purification to conform to the image of Christ that is our spirit man; a meek and quiet spirit cannot be corrupted. This is what God hid in those who believe:

1 Peter 3:4
4 But let it be **the hidden man of the heart, in that which is not corruptible, even the ornament of a meek and quiet spirit**, which is in the sight of God of great price.
KJV

Life for men is our flesh being alive, but life for God is spiritual life. Christ told a follower to come with Him and let the dead bury the dead. He was talking about the spiritually dead should bury the man who had physically died. Christ came to quicken our spirit, which means to bring it back to spiritual life connecting us to the Father. We are to walk upright in righteousness before God.

Rom 8:11-14
11 But if the Spirit of him that raised up Jesus from the dead dwell in you, **he that raised up Christ from the dead shall also quicken your mortal bodies by his Spirit that dwelleth in you.**
12 Therefore, brethren, we are debtors, not to the flesh, to live after the flesh.
13 **For if ye live after the flesh, ye shall die: but if ye through the Spirit do mortify the deeds of the body, ye shall live.**
14 **For as many as are led by the Spirit of God, they are the sons of God.** (KJV)

Even though God quickens our spirit and His Spirit and ours becomes one, until you submit to God's rule you are still walking in the flesh. You are still walking as a beast. Christ said, "Father, not Mine will but let Thine will be done." Ask yourself if you are walking in the image of Christ or the image of the beast. Who is your head, you, or Christ?

God in us is Christ in us, which is when the Holy Spirit and our spirit become one. When we obey God we are allowing the Holy Spirit to rule in us, and that is when we no longer walk as beasts but upright as men. **The true meaning of walking in the Spirit, and not in the flesh, is to allow God to rule in our lives.** God created Adam upright. Scripture confirms this as true.

Eccl 7:29
29 Lo, this only have I found, that **God hath made man upright**; but they have sought out **many inventions**.
KJV

God created man upright with a heart to obey Him but we have gone after our own inventions. We justify doing our own will by trying to say God has no problem with it, even when His Word reveals that He does. When Adam and Eve sinned against God, they died spiritually. They became just like beasts with only a functional soul and flesh but spiritually they were dead. God could have made any type of clothes to give them when He expelled them from the garden, but he gave them animal skins because they were spiritually not walking upright according to How God created them. They were walking in the flesh as beasts.

When Nebuchadnezzar was humbled and realized that His kingdom was given by God and that He is the true ruler over all men, then God lifted him up as a man. His experience teaches us that when we submit to God, we no longer walk as a beast in the desires of the flesh and the carnal mind. **Nebuchadnezzar's experience was a lesson to us all that when we humble ourselves, see God as the true ruler, and then submit to Him, we walk upright as men and not beasts.**

Do you realize that faith means to obey God? Faith is belief in God's Word (His promises). The evidence of your belief is walking according to that Word. You cannot say you have faith and then refuse to obey. Belief is walking according to God's truth.

Hab 2:4
4 Behold, **his soul which is lifted up is not upright in him: but the just shall live by his faith.**
KJV

People often talk about personality traits such as pride, self, anger, lust, fear, etc. These are the soulish parts of mankind. The Holy Spirit cannot rule in a person that allows the flesh or the soulish nature to rule. Those who do this are not upright they are walking as beasts. Their head is not on top. Their head is not in charge. Remember Christ is our head ruling through our spirit.

Ps 18:23-28
23 **I was also upright before him, and I kept myself from mine iniquity.**
24 Therefore hath the LORD recompensed me according to my righteousness, according to the cleanness of my hands in his eyesight.
25 With the merciful thou wilt shew thyself merciful; with an upright man thou wilt shew thyself upright;
26 With the pure thou wilt shew thyself pure; and with the froward thou wilt shew thyself froward.
27 For thou wilt save the afflicted people; but wilt bring down high looks.
28 **For thou wilt light my candle: the LORD my God will enlighten my darkness.**
KJV

Do you realize that "light my candle" is a metaphor for bringing your spirit to life? The responsibility of your spirit is to search out your soul (belly) and flesh to find everything that does not belong so God can remove it. Your spirit along with the Holy Spirit searches for pride, lust, covetousness, hatred, anger, violence, jealousy, fear, etc. When these things are found within us, along with the demonic spirits that attach to these personality traits, we petition God to have them removed.

Prov 20:27
27 **The spirit of man** is the candle of the LORD, searching all the inward parts of the belly.
KJV

When we allow Christ to rule in us, His responsibility is to take us through the process of mortifying (killing) the flesh and transforming the soul into the image of Christ. This can only occur if we allow Christ to be our head. **Real salvation is allowing God to rule.**

Titus 2:11-14
11 For the grace of God that bringeth salvation hath appeared to all men,
12 Teaching us that, denying ungodliness and worldly lusts, we should live soberly, righteously, and godly, in this present world;
13 Looking for that blessed hope, and the glorious appearing of the great God and our Saviour Jesus Christ;
14 Who gave himself for us, that he might redeem us from all iniquity, and **purify unto himself a peculiar people**, zealous of good works.
KJV

I want you to understand that this is systematic in Christ's Kingdom. God has appointed family relationships in accordance with the heavenly relationships. Christ has the Father as his head, and He submits to the Father's will in all things. Christ is the head of the church and man in the same fashion. In family relationships, God has placed the man as the head according to this same principle.

1 Cor 11:3
3 But I would have you know, that **the head of every man is Christ; and the head of the woman is the man; and the head of Christ is God.**
KJV.

To walk upright is to say, "Father not my will, but let your will be done." This is the lesson Christ ministered to us from the garden of Gethsemane where He showed that through humility to the Father's will we become strong.

The devil does everything to attack this image. He tried to remove the Father as the head of Christ when he offered Christ all the kingdoms of the world to bow down and worship him.

Matt 4:8-10
8 Again, the devil taketh him up into an exceeding high mountain, and sheweth him all the kingdoms of the world, and the glory of them;
9 And saith unto him, **All these things will I give thee, if thou wilt fall down and worship me.**
10 Then saith Jesus unto him, Get thee hence, Satan: for **it is written, Thou shalt worship the Lord thy God, and him only shalt thou serve.**
KJV

He tricked Adam and Eve into rejecting God as their head by saying they could be their own gods. The world pushes this same agenda by insisting that a man is not the head of the family. There are subliminal messages pushed through the entertainment industry that women are to rule the world. The message to the family is that the woman is really in charge. The system that God has set up is being rearranged in a direct rejection of God. Even the children are being taught that it is okay to rebel against their parents and make their own decisions. Do we realize that our relationships and family structure teaches us to submit to God? We are given 70 years or more as a blessing. If we refuse to do it God's way, for this oh so limited amount of time, who is going to trust us with eternity? The most beautiful thing in a family is to see a man submitted to Christ, a woman submitted to her husband, and children submitted to their parents. God knows, and we should understand this truth, that if we cannot submit in this limited time on earth we will never submit in heaven. We will walk in the image of Satan and want to rule in God's place. We will become like beasts.

Satan's trick is to assure us that it is ok to DO THINE OWN WILL. I remember seeing an interview with a rapper (Hip Hop rapper) who has shown in many ways his allegiance to everything against God. His videos are full of subliminal messages that show his disdain for the Kingdom of God and expose his loyalty to the kingdom of this world (Satan's kingdom). This man has confessed that he is going to destroy the Christian church in his music. During the interview, he was wearing a t-shirt that read, "Do thine own will." Most viewers had no idea that this saying came from a book written by a warlock and Satan worshipper (I will not name the book). The saying is anti-word, which is antichrist. It is an attack against Christ's own Words, "Nevertheless not my will, but thine be done."

Luke 22:42-43
42 Saying, Father, if thou be willing, remove this cup from me: **nevertheless not my will, but thine, be done.**
43 And there appeared an angel unto him from heaven, **strengthening him.**
KJV

Some may wonder what this has to do with the image of the beast. Please be patient as we go through this process. It is imperative that you understand what Christ was doing and saying because it shines the light on what the image of the beast really is.

Christ was not tempted to go against the Father's will when He said, "Not my will, but thine, be done." He told the apostles to, "Watch and pray," but watch what, and pray for what? It was nighttime, and they were in a garden on the Mount of Olives. He already knew the authorities were coming for Him and when they would get there, so what did He want the Apostles to watch for? Christ wanted the apostles to watch Him and then pray the words He was going to pray. He knew that they would be tempted to give up and would need to do exactly what He was showing them. Read carefully:

Matt 26:36-44
36 Then cometh Jesus with them unto a place called Gethsemane, and saith unto the disciples, Sit ye here, while I go and pray yonder.
37 And **he took with him Peter and the two sons of Zebedee, and began to be sorrowful and very heavy.**
38 Then saith he unto them, My soul is exceeding sorrowful, even unto death: tarry ye here, and watch with me.
39 And he went a little further, and fell on his face, and prayed, saying, O my Father, **if it be possible, let this cup pass from me: nevertheless not as I will, but as thou wilt.**

Image of the Beast

40 And he cometh unto the disciples, and findeth them asleep, and saith unto Peter, What, could ye not watch with me one hour?

41 **Watch and pray, that ye enter not into temptation: the spirit indeed is willing, but the flesh is weak.**

42 He went away again the second time, and prayed, saying, O my Father, if this cup may not pass away from me, except I drink it, thy will be done.

43 And he came and found them asleep again: for their eyes were heavy.

44 And he left them, and went away again, and **prayed the third time, saying the same words.**

KJV

Christ told the disciples to pray that they do not enter into temptation. Luke noted in his version of the story that an angel came and strengthened Christ. Christ told them their flesh was weak, they needed strengthening. We as believers have to watch what Christ did and learn from it. Do you realize that most people pray after they have gone through the temptation and have already failed? Have you ever wondered if Peter would have followed Jesus' instructions and prayed as Jesus prayed that perhaps he would have been strengthened also, and able to stand by Jesus' side rather than denying him and fleeing? Prayer to the Father is a form of humbling ourselves, even as we bow down and acknowledge Him as the true and living God. We say, "Father not our will but let your will be done," then He will send an angel to strengthen us so that we also can have the ability to do what He has willed for us to do. God's will and not being led into temptation is in the format given on how to pray (Matt 6:9-13)

When we submit to God's will, we acknowledge Him as our head, and He lifts us up so we can walk upright. We are no longer beasts walking according to our carnal desires. We become what God has created us to be.

The beast of Revelation is the Roman Empire, but why would God call them a beast? Is there hidden wisdom in the use of the metaphor of "beast" for the nations in the books of Daniel and Revelation? Is God trying to teach us something specific about these nations in contrast to Nebuchadnezzar and Babylon? Let's go a little deeper.

God Hated Them

Hos 9:15

15 All **their wickedness is in Gilgal: for there I hated them**: for the wickedness of their doings I will drive them out of mine house, **I will love them no more**: all their princes are revolters.
KJV

Why did God hate them? Why would God say, about Israel, "I will love them no more"? What could Israel have done that was so horrible that God literally said He was going to put them out of His house? It was at Gilgal that Israel as a nation became a beast.

Even though, many people have read the verse from Hosea 9:15, where God confesses His loss of love for Israel, not many have taken the time to find out exactly what Israel did. Many have assumed but we do not have that luxury when dealing with such a serious matter. Please place the key in the time machine; we need to take another trip.

We are touching down around 1425 bce. Yes, we have gone way back. The place is Gilgal as it has just been named by God. We hear the rushing of waters and realize that Gilgal is located right by the river Jordan. You do not realize it but we are standing in one of the most important locations in the scriptures. This is the very spot where Israel crossed over into the Promised Land. If you look down by the river you can see 12 stones set up as a memorial to mark this site where Israel crossed over. We just missed them, but let me explain to you what happened here.

We missed one of the greatest miracles that God performed through Joshua. When they arrived at the banks of the Jordan, God split the waters and the Jordan River rolled back in the same manner as the Red Sea. The Ark of the Covenant carried by the priests was sent to the middle of the river. The priests stood still as millions of Israelites passed by walking through a great hallway of water. They knew that their God was with them. Forty years they had wandered through the wilderness. God had kept His promise that no one but Caleb and Joshua, of those who were twenty years and older, would enter the land (those who murmured against God, would not). Everyone else who feared and refused to enter the Promised Land initially as God had instructed died. It took forty years as one by one, all of the adults dropped dead in the wilderness. Even Moses and Aaron found their graves on the wrong side of the Jordan.

One after another, the Israelites streamed across the dried riverbed and stepped on the other side of the Jordan. God honored His promise and took His people into the Promised Land. This was such an important event that God instructed Joshua to have one leader from each tribe go back into the Jordan. Each one would remove a large stone, one for each of the 12 tribes, and set them up as a memorial to remind the future generations of the event. God also had Joshua circumcise all the males because while they had wandered in the wilderness the practice was not kept. Circumcision was the sign between God and the descendants of Abraham, the covenant signature. By suspending this practice for the 40 years of wandering, it revealed that the whole nation was in a state of reproach.

After God had Joshua do the rituals, He kept Israel in the same place until they kept the Passover as a memorial of them being delivered from Egypt. What many people miss is that God named the place Gilgal, which means "wheel" in Hebrew. The name was given because it was the location where God **rolled away** the reproach of the nation. They were brought back into good standing with God.

Gilgal became a very famous and important place to the tribes of Israel. In the early years of the nation, an altar was set up there, and it was a type of capital while Israel warred to take the Promised Land. Yet, this was the same place where God would confess that He turned to hate them and would love them no more. That is a very powerful statement given by God through the prophet Hosea.

I am always amazed at how God has a way of hiding things right in front of us. I have often used Hosea 9:15 to open up the understanding of believers who teach God's continual love is unconditional. I can't even count how many times I have heard this and just shook my head wishing people would teach what scripture says, and not add their private interpretation. We receive God's love without condition on our belief in Christ but we keep His love with condition that we love Christ and keep His commandments. **If,** is a powerful word! Many people seem to not understand that "if" itself sets a condition. We know God loved us first and sent His Son to die for us, but there are conditions to maintaining and retaining that love. Christ said if we love Him we should want to keep the commandments He left with us. He calls this abiding in Him! He expounds on the fact that keeping His commandments is abiding in His love. He is not talking about the Law of Moses or even the Ten Commandments; He is speaking of His doctrine that He was sent with from the Father to give to the church:

John 14:23-24
23 Jesus answered and said unto him, **If a man love me, he will keep my words**: and my Father will love him, and we will come unto him, and make our abode with him.
24 He that loveth me not keepeth not my sayings: **and the word which ye hear is not mine, but the Father's which sent me.**
KJV

Christ also shows we can walk out of His love

John 15:9-10
9 As the Father hath loved me, so have I loved you: **continue ye in my love.**
10 If ye keep my commandments, ye shall abide in my love; even as I have kept my Father's commandments, and abide in his love. (KJV)

This statement alone shows there are conditions to staying in Christ and the Father's love. This is confirmed by what was spoken by Hosea. God hated them because of their wickedness.

However, what did Israel do?

Let's jump back into the time machine and move ahead a few hundred years to about 1150 ce. We need to see how Israel got their first king. We are going to be touching down in a town called Ramah in Israel. Israel through the help of God has taken the Promised Land. Anytime that God needs a leader He raises up a judge to lead the people into battle and bring judgment in certain situations. There is no dispute that God is still the ruler. Those He raises up are to do His will with the help of the priests, the descendants of Aaron. Things are about to change.

THE REIGN OF KINGS
(To be like the world)

The nation of Israel decided they wanted to be just like all the other nations. They requested for Samuel, who had been a judge over them for many years, to appoint them a king. Samuel thought it was a bad decision but still inquired of God on the subject. God saw what Samuel did not see in the heart of the people. They wanted a king so God would not rule over them. They were not rejecting Samuel; they were rejecting God:

1 Sam 8:4-7
4 Then all **the elders of Israel** gathered themselves together, and came to Samuel unto Ramah,
5 And said unto him, Behold, thou art old, and thy sons walk not in thy ways: now **make us a king to judge us like all the nations.**
6 But the thing displeased Samuel, when they said, Give us a king to judge us. And Samuel prayed unto the LORD.
7 And the LORD said unto Samuel, Hearken unto the voice of the people in all that they say unto thee: **for they have not rejected thee, but they have rejected me, that I should not reign over them.**
(KJV)

When God spoke to Samuel and said, "They have not rejected thee, they have rejected me," He was speaking of how the people blatantly rejected God's rule so they could have a man rule over them (like other nations). The people said they wanted to be like the other nations, but God saw in their hearts that it was a direct rejection of His rule. By setting up a king, the people allowed a man to usurp God's rightful position. A man would rule over the people and this was the greatest sin. This was the sin of Gilgal where God hated Israel. God said all their princes had rebelled, and He was speaking of a specific event that the leaders of the twelve tribes had perpetrated:

Hos 9:15
15 All their wickedness is in Gilgal: for there I hated them: for the wickedness of their doings I will drive them out of mine house, **I will love them no more: all their princes are revolters.**
KJV

  I want you to just sit quietly in the time machine and just listen (read) to the dialogue between God, Samuel, and the people.

1 Sam 8:8-22
8 According to all the works which they have done since the day that I brought them up out of Egypt even unto this day, **wherewith they have forsaken me**, and served other gods, so do they also unto thee.
9 Now therefore hearken unto their voice: **howbeit yet protest solemnly unto them, and shew them the manner of the king that shall reign over them.**
10 And Samuel told all the words of the LORD unto the people that asked of him a king.
11 And he said, This will be the manner of the king that shall reign over you: He will take your sons, and appoint them for himself, for his chariots, and to be his horsemen; and some shall run before his chariots.
12 And he will appoint him captains over thousands, and captains over fifties; and will set them to ear his ground, and to reap his harvest, and to make his instruments of war, and instruments of his chariots.
13 And he will take your daughters to be confectionaries, and to be cooks, and to be bakers.
14 And he will take your fields, and your vineyards, and your oliveyards, even the best of them, and give them to his servants.
15 And he will take the tenth of your seed, and of your vineyards, and give to his officers, and to his servants.
16 And he will take your menservants, and your maidservants, and your goodliest young men, and your asses, and put them to his work.
17 He will take the tenth of your sheep: and ye shall be his servants.
18 And ye shall cry out in that day because of your king which ye shall have chosen you; and the LORD will not hear you in that day.
19 Nevertheless the people refused to obey the voice of Samuel; and they said, Nay; but we will have a king over us;

20 That we also may be like all the nations; and that our king may judge us, and go out before us, and fight our battles.
21 And Samuel heard all the words of the people, and he rehearsed them in the ears of the LORD.
22 And the LORD said to Samuel, Hearken unto their voice, and make them a king. And Samuel said unto the men of Israel, Go ye every man unto his city.
KJV

I can see the sadness in your eyes. Despite all God has done for these people in bringing them out of slavery, and giving them such a wonderful land with houses and towns that they did not build, yet still they reject Him so they can rule over themselves. Samuel understood the consequences, but the people did not comprehend the fullness of their decision. What makes it even sadder is that God instructed Samuel to tell the people just how the king they wanted for themselves would abuse them, steal from them, utilize their sons and daughters for his purposes, and appoint other men who would also abuse them; nevertheless they still wanted their king.

Doesn't this sound familiar to you? No, I am not talking about what our leaders do today, even though it is true they do the same. I am talking about how God brought us out of the bondage of sin. Nevertheless, in many cases we as His people do not really want Him to rule in our lives but will allow pride, covetousness, lust, and other fleshly (soulish) desires to rule over us instead of God. We as a people will see how the world operates and want to do the same things they do. We want to act like them, dress like them, speak like them, and mingle with them. We want to learn their ways and then try to justify it as we stand before God and His Word. Aren't we sometimes just like Israel? Thank God for Christ and the mercy seat.

Let's head back to the time machine. Don't worry, we are not going too far, just a few days into the future, back to Gilgal. God is going to give Israel a king after their own heart (wicked), and He is going to instruct Samuel to take this king, a young man named Saul, right back to the place where the people swore allegiance to God as they entered the Promised Land. The place where they set up memorial markers to remember all that God had done for them.
1 Sam 11:14-15

14 Then said Samuel to the people, Come, and **let us go to Gilgal, and renew the kingdom there.**
15 And all the people went to Gilgal; and there they made Saul king before the LORD in Gilgal; and there they sacrificed sacrifices of peace offerings before the LORD; and there **Saul and all the men of Israel rejoiced greatly.**
KJV

We stare in disbelief as the people are rejoicing. I wonder if they realize that Samuel is not rejoicing with them. He is an old man now with sadness in his eyes. It reminds me of Moses after God had shown him the future of the nation of Israel. They would turn away to wickedness and their own devices. Let's continue watching:

1 Sam 12:1-25
12:1 And Samuel said unto all Israel, Behold, I have hearkened unto your voice in all that ye said unto me, and have made a king over you.
2 And now, behold, the king walketh before you: and I am old and grayheaded; and, behold, my sons are with you: and I have walked before you from my childhood unto this day.
3 Behold, here I am: witness against me before the LORD, and before his anointed: whose ox have I taken? or whose ass have I taken? or whom have I defrauded? whom have I oppressed? or of whose hand have I received any bribe to blind mine eyes therewith? and I will restore it you.
4 And they said, Thou hast not defrauded us, nor oppressed us, neither hast thou taken ought of any man's hand.
5 And he said unto them, The LORD is witness against you, and his anointed is witness this day, that ye have not found ought in my hand. And they answered, He is witness.
6 And Samuel said unto the people, It is the LORD that advanced Moses and Aaron, and that brought your fathers up out of the land of Egypt.
7 Now therefore stand still, that I may reason with you before the LORD of all the righteous acts of the LORD, which he did to you and to your fathers.
8 When Jacob was come into Egypt, and your fathers cried unto the LORD, then the LORD sent Moses and Aaron, which brought forth your fathers out of Egypt, and made them dwell in this place.

9 And when they forgat the LORD their God, he sold them into the hand of Sisera, captain of the host of Hazor, and into the hand of the Philistines, and into the hand of the king of Moab, and they fought against them.

10 And they cried unto the LORD, and said, We have sinned, because we have forsaken the LORD, and have served Baalim and Ashtaroth: but now deliver us out of the hand of our enemies, and we will serve thee.

11 And the LORD sent Jerubbaal, and Bedan, and Jephthah, and Samuel, and delivered you out of the hand of your enemies on every side, and ye dwelled safe.

12 And when ye saw that Nahash the king of the children of Ammon came against you, **ye said unto me, Nay; but a king shall reign over us: when the LORD your God was your king.**

13 Now therefore behold the king whom ye have chosen, and whom ye have desired! and, behold, the LORD hath set a king over you.

14 If ye will fear the LORD, and serve him, and obey his voice, and not rebel against the commandment of the LORD, then shall both ye and also the king that reigneth over you continue following the LORD your God:

15 But if ye will not obey the voice of the LORD, but rebel against the commandment of the LORD, then shall the hand of the LORD be against you, as it was against your fathers.

16 Now therefore stand and see this great thing, which the LORD will do before your eyes.

17 Is it not wheat harvest to day? I will call unto the LORD, and he shall send thunder and rain; that ye may perceive and see that your wickedness is great, which ye have done in the sight of the LORD, in asking you a king.

18 So Samuel called unto the LORD; and the LORD sent thunder and rain that day: and all the people greatly feared the LORD and Samuel.

19 And all **the people said unto Samuel, Pray for thy servants unto the LORD thy God, that we die not: for we have added unto all our sins this evil, to ask us a king.**

20 And Samuel said unto the people, Fear not: ye have done all this wickedness: yet turn not aside from following the LORD, but serve the LORD with all your heart;

21 And **turn ye not aside: for then should ye go after vain things, which cannot profit nor deliver; for they are vain.**

22 For the LORD will not forsake his people for his great name's sake: because it hath pleased the LORD to make you his people.

23 Moreover as for me, God forbid that I should sin against the LORD in ceasing to pray for you: but I will teach you the good and the right way:

24 Only fear the LORD, and serve him in truth with all your heart: for consider how great things he hath done for you.

25 **But if ye shall still do wickedly, ye shall be consumed, both ye and your king.**

KJV

The people were rejoicing because they were just like the rest of the world with a king over them. **They did not realize that being like the world is the first step in sharing the world's destiny.** God knew it would go from God's rule, to a king's rule, and finally to people's rule. Let's break it down.

When God rules a nation it is like the Holy Spirit residing in a man's spirit and is ruling. When a king that does not have God as his head rules, it is like the soul ruling, which is not the purpose of the soul because the soul is not a ruler it is a facilitator. The facilitator does not have the strength to rule and will soon be overcome by the people (flesh). A kingship that is not occupied by God or a true man of God will be overthrown by the people. The people will usurp the rule of the king's position by themselves or with the help of others and will control the country. In the same way when the soul rules, the flesh will usurp that rule. What was going on with Israel is a reflection of what we go through in our Christian walk. We have the same fight with the flesh as we as souls decide if we will follow the Spirit.

The flesh will gain control by itself or with the help of outside forces (demons). There will be a coup. Show me a country with a godless kingdom rule, and I will show you a country that eventually will be overthrown. Show me a carnal minded Christian that allows his soul to rule, and I will show you a Christian that is about to be overthrown and ruled by his flesh.

In the same manner when Christ is ruling in a person the person is stable and accepted by God. When the carnal soul of a man is ruling it will be usurped by the flesh. The flesh can't overthrow the spirit. It has to get the soul to follow it instead of following the spirit man, which is Christ in you. Once the flesh gets the soul to follow it, the soul will be brought into bondage (overthrown). In the end, the flesh and the forces that dwell in the flesh will rule. Satan could not overthrow God. He had to deceive one third of the angels to follow him. He is now ruling over them. They are following him straight to hell and are trying to recruit us to take the same ride.

The people want a king to rule because they know he actually cannot rule unless they allow him. The king can be manipulated but God cannot. That is why kings gather others under themselves to help control the people. As long as you make these others rich, they will help control the masses. God knew what the outcome would be. Countries that are like beasts: in the end will be ruled by the wicked desires of the king and people. This is what happened to the Roman Empire, they had the image of self-rule and it consumed them.

We jump in the time machine. We are back to the present with a lot to think about. We now understand what the mark is, which we are told not to get, and have a better understanding of what the image of the beast is, which is self-rule. We now realize that the image of the beast, when talking about a country, will be the type of government that is ruling the people. Let's take a look at the last scripture dealing with the image.

Rev 13:11-18
11 And I beheld **another beast coming up out of the earth**; and he had **two horns like a lamb, and he spake as a dragon.**
12 And he **exerciseth all the power of the first beast** before him, and **causeth the earth and them which dwell therein to worship the first beast, whose deadly wound was healed.**
13 And he doeth great wonders, so that **he maketh fire come down from heaven on the earth in the sight of men,**
14 And deceiveth them that dwell on the earth by the means of those miracles which he had power to do in the sight of the beast; saying to them that dwell on the earth, that they should **make an image to the beast, which had the wound by a sword, and did live.**

15 And he had **power to give life unto the image of the beast,** that **the image of the beast should both speak,** and cause that **as many as would not worship the image of the beast should be killed.**
16 And he causeth all, both small and great, rich and poor, free and bond, to receive a mark in their right hand, or in their foreheads:
17 And that no man might buy or sell, save he that had the mark, or the name of the beast, or the number of his name.
18 Here is wisdom. Let him that hath understanding count the number of the beast: for it is the number of a man; and his number is Six hundred threescore and six.
KJV

Here we have another beast coming up out of the earth and not the sea. It is coming up out of the earth and not the sea because it is not a multitude of people forming a country, it is a group of people from a country forming another. This beast, which we know is a country, will be linked to the first beast, which is Rome. This beast has two horns like a lamb, which means it will have two areas of power. Yet it speaks like a dragon. This country will have all authority like Rome so we know it will be a superpower. It will not be just any country. It will be a country that has extreme control over our modern world. This country will form an organization that will push self-rule and will promote this all across the globe.

The image of the beast is the government of Rome. Earlier in the book, we spoke of the Roman initialism of SPQR, which meant the people and senate of Rome (flesh and soul). Rome was a republic that transformed into an empire. They had a history of people fighting for power to include assassinations and civil wars. The second beast (country) that speaks like a dragon (the devil) will be pushing this same type of government to the rest of the world. This image will be propagated by the second beast of Revelation.

There will come a time when almost all if not all the governments of the world will have the same image as Rome, or one close to it. All will claim that their government is for the people but in reality, it will set the stage for Satan to have total control (as God allows) over all nations. People will try to fight this but it will be a losing cause. What is written must be. Our job as Christians is to do everything possible to spread the gospel, and save as many people as we can, because it will all come to a head when Christ returns to bring judgment to this wicked world. We have to believe this and walk in faith. The pressure to accept the things of the world will be enormous, and the persecution against those who refuse to take the mark and image of Rome is going to grow.

This is why giving up Christmas is such a hard challenge, because you have to make a choice. Christ could have found a thousand reasons why He did not have to die. He could have come up with so many other ways to save mankind but instead He said, "Father not my will but let thy will be done." He was setting an example for us. We are going to have the same choice. The flesh is of this world, and if we allow it to rule, it will enslave the soul to sin. Sin is of the world and the fate of the world is sealed. The way of the world is self-willed, self-love, self-rule, self-preservation, self-help, and self-everything. The world says, "I am going to do me." When will we say, "Father not my will but let your will be done"? When are we going to let go of the image of the beast?

Witches know

She was a young lady that was invited many years ago to the Bible study I teach. I remember she was very energetic a tongues speaking born again Christian. She was so inquisitive and eager to learn. I had already begun to notice that those being guided to the Bible study by the Holy Spirit were individuals that had been hurt in some way in their Christian walk and needed building up. I knew eventually God would reveal her issues and it would be addressed in the teachings. The other members had mentioned to her that I had taught on Christmas, and it was an eye opener. She would ask me about it but I would tell her to be patient and learn the things that make up the foundation of Christ's doctrine and then we would get to the deeper things.

At this time, I was in a spiritual struggle with the church I was attending. The Bible study group I taught in my parents home had started to grow quickly. The church leadership was afraid I was planning on starting my own church and drawing away members from them. The pastor actually brought me into a meeting and told me he would help me to start a church but just for me to be patient. I told him God did not tell me anything about starting a church or being a pastor. He just told me to teach. I assured them on more than one occasion that this was not my intention, but to no avail. They attempted to do something to discredit me, so they started telling everyone that I did not celebrate Christmas. What was perplexing was that the pastor had assured me Christmas was just a tradition and would in no way affect my standing in the church. However, when individuals in different departments wanted to utilize me to minister in some way, they were told not to use me. When they asked, what the problem was if I was walking contrary to the church teaching. They were told that I did not celebrate Christmas. The Bible study continued to grow and I was ordered by the pastor to stop the Bible study. The Bible study group and I fasted to get instructions from God because I was commanded by Him to do the Bible study, and I did not want to obey man and disobey God. God answered me in a way that I would have no doubt.

It was Sunday morning service, and one of the head deacons asked me to stand up while I was seated in the congregation. I remember grabbing my Bible and saying to myself, "Just walk out and don't make a scene." I was sure they were going to ask me to leave the church. I was shocked at what happened next. The deacon said God had given him a message for me while he was praying before church. He said, "You want to stop doing what God has called you to do because of people." He then instructed me that I must do what God told me to do despite what men wanted. The Bible study members started praising God, and I burst out in praise and worship. I looked over and the Pastor was sitting with his head down in disbelief. After the service, I asked the pastor if I should accept the word that came forth. He said that it was between me and the prophet that brought the word, it had nothing to do with him. He still wanted me to stop the Bible study. I told him that I was not going to stop because I was going to obey God before men.

After church, the deacon asked me what was going on, because he did not know what the word he brought was about. I told him that the pastor wanted me to stop the Bible study that God had instructed me to do. He told me with tears in his eyes that other members of the leadership that knew what was going on came to him and were very upset because of the word he received. He also advised me that his plan was to talk to me in private, but the Holy Spirit told him to say it in the front of the church. Even though he was not scheduled to be the moderator for the morning service they advised him that something happened with the person who was supposed to moderate and they asked him to do it. He realized it was God's doing so that he could bring the message before the church. I thought the opposition would have come to an end after that but the truth is, all hell broke loose. The next time I spoke to the deacon, he had tears in his eyes because members of the leadership had basically turned against him just because he did what God told him to do. I started having all sorts of spiritual attacks. Members of the Bible study who attended the church (some did not) were told if they attended the Bible study then they would be in rebellion against the church. This was some of the hardest years of my Christian walk. I would later find out that many of the members of the church were involved in witchcraft. What was even sadder was many of the other members knew this and were reluctant to expose it.

It was around this time when the young lady spoken about earlier started to attend the bible study. She was not a member of the church. She had a best friend who was a minister that she confided with. She would share the things she was learning in the Bible study with him. He called my pastor to get more information about me and was told that I was in rebellion against church leadership and that I didn't celebrate Christmas. The minister told the young lady to leave the Bible study, sadly she did. I advised her to make sure wherever she was, she should find a group of people who loved the Lord and continue studying the Bible.

Before she left, she had shared an experience where she was approached by a man in a store who knew she was a Christian even though he did not know her. Come to find out, the man who struck up a conversation with her, and wanted to get to know her, was a warlock and attended the same church I was going to. During the time I was there, God had revealed to me that the church had a large group of people who practiced witchcraft and were actually wolves in sheep's clothing. I shared the information with the pastor and even gave him the names of the people God had shown me but absolutely nothing was done. The man was one of the names on the list.

I did not think it was a coincidence that this man approached the young lady. I believed he saw something in her that identified her as easy prey. I truly believe this was the reason she was sent to the Bible study because a strong part of my ministry is spiritual warfare and exposing the tricks of the enemy. She never got the chance to receive the instructions and deliverance that she needed.

A couple years later, the Bible study member who had invited the young lady to the Bible study gave me some shocking news. The young lady contacted her and advised her she was living in New York. She then gleefully let her know that she was one-step from becoming a witch. She had rejected Christianity and gone over to the occult. Then she said something that was even more shocking. She told the member that I was right all the time about Christmas because she had learned that Christmas really had nothing to do with Christ, it was theirs.

I had tears in my eyes. Not because she found out the truth about Christmas from the wrong source, it was because this could have all been prevented if people would just have allowed the young lady to stay where she was being taught the truth. I was extremely angry with my old pastor, and the pastor that was the friend of the young woman. It took a while before I could release this anger. Where were these people while she was being recruited to this wickedness? This was not the first time that I have seen Christians recruited into witchcraft, but this was personal. The enemy's devices are not new and can easily be thwarted with the teaching of the truth. Yet so many churches are so busy preaching about money and the blessings that they are not aware that their churches have been infiltrated by workers of the occult. They are not just recruiting outside the church; they are recruiting from the inside. The truth about Christmas that many in the church refuse to hear is well known by the workers of iniquity. The devil's kingdom knows whose birthday is really on the 25th of December, while we are still sleeping.

Chapter 10

Camouflaged in Christmas

I want to put away the time machine for now so we can look at some of the symbols of Christmas from the world's standpoint, and expose how the enemy of our souls has camouflaged himself under a false covering of good. We have already looked at the religious beliefs, but now we are going to look at the things of the world dealing with Christmas from a secular standpoint. The devil has cleverly presented himself and the things of his kingdom in disguise. It is almost like a math problem, where if you want to get the answer you have to reduce the problem to the lowest common denominator. You have to look at simple things that link all the false gods and pagan traditions together in order to find the common ground. Once you find the common ground, it is easy to expose the common source.

Satan = Santa

It is just a little play on letters. When you take the name Santa, take the N, and move it to the end, it spells out the name Satan. This is common knowledge but let's compare the two. Do you realize that another name of the devil is Old Nick? It comes from the German word nickel. Now get this, the German word nickel means Satan. This is where the name Old Nick for the devil comes from. While in college, I took a chemistry class and was surprised to find out that the element nickel got its name from the German word for devil. I was even more surprised to discover that nickel as a metal often has a red hue and that is why the Germans (who discovered the element) named it after the devil. What color do you think about when you think of Satan? Red! Remember that old red devil, now picture Santa. Are you starting to get the picture? The color red is common ground along with the name Nick. So far it seems like circumstantial evidence but it gets more interesting.

In addition, there is a saint in the Christian Church named St. Nicholas. He ties into the history of Santa also. St. Nicholas was the bishop of Myra, a city in turkey (modern-day Demre) around the 3rd century. He was known for his miracles and secret giving of gifts. Originally, St. Nicholas was in no way linked to the winter solstice or Christmas. Over the years as the tradition developed, Christmas time stores in Europe told of him going around during the winter solstice bringing presents to good children. If you want to poison someone, you can't give them a cup of cyanide. They will never drink it. But if you mix the cyanide into a cup of Kool-Aid (a sweet drink), then you can deceive a person into drinking the poison. The tradition of Santa being based on St. Nicholas is the Kool-Aide, but the truth of who he is really based on is the cyanide.

Long before Santa Clause, Sinterklaas, Father Christmas, and all the other representations of the gift giver of Christmas, there was another person whose characteristics are a perfect match for Santa. He is the first person to come into homes through a hole in the roof. In the northern countries of what is now Europe, long before Christianity, they worshiped the false god Odin (Woden). Odin was described as an old man with white hair and a long white beard. He was the head Norse god whose son is the Marvel superhero of today named Thor. Odin would bring gifts on the winter solstice and enter the homes through smokestacks and holes in the roof. He was also known to ride a reindeer. You might be thinking why does Santa being based on Odin make him the cyanide. It would seem that it would be no different from St. Nicholas. My question to you is, "If he is not the cyanide, then why do they hide and disguise the fact of who Santa really is?" The Bible says Satan is going to deceive the whole world, and in truth, most worship him through deception. Let's look deep into the cyanide. Take a long look at the depiction of the false god Odin by Georg Von Rosen (1886) below. Do you notice anything missing?

Yes, you got it. Odin like Horus the Egyptian sun god only has one eye. That eye on the pyramid from the dollar sure has a lot of people who can claim it.

I want you to understand that all of these gods are linked together in some form or fashion because the people who worship them are also all linked together. The Bible says all men are created from one blood:

Acts 17:26
26 And hath made of **one blood all nations of men** for to dwell on all the face of the earth, and hath determined the times before appointed, and the bounds of their habitation;
KJV

We can all trace our ancestors back to Adam. We are all related to the eight people who came out of the ark after the flood. We are all related to Noah. The first man worshiped as a god was Nimrod, Noah's great-grandson, and almost all myths in some way can be traced back to this one man. When God destroyed the tower of Babel and scattered men all around the earth to form individual nations, they all held the stories of the flood, ark, and first men worshipped as gods.

Gen 11:8-9
8 So the **LORD scattered them abroad** from thence upon the face of all the earth: and they left off to build the city.
9 Therefore is the name of it called Babel; because the LORD did there **confound the language of all the earth: and from thence did the LORD scatter them abroad** upon the face of all the earth.
KJV

Over the millenniums, the stories were added to, retold, warped, and reshaped to fit the developing cultures. We have to remember that the writers of the Bible were men writing under the inspiration of God. Moses himself who wrote the first five books received the history of the world from the angels who witnessed what occurred.

Acts 7:53
53 Who have received the law by **the disposition of angels**, and have not kept it.
KJV

The change in languages caused the change in the names of these men worshipped as gods. All these stories have common factors that still allow us to link them together to illustrate their common source. It is not a coincidence that both Odin and Horus have an eye missing. Just like it is not a coincidence that almost all nations have a flood story.

We also have to remember that Satan was ruling this world (as God allowed because of the wickedness of men). He showed Christ, during His temptation in the wilderness, all the nations of the world in a vision and indicated he had possession of them.

Luke 4:5-6
5 And the devil, taking him up into an high mountain, **shewed unto him all the kingdoms of the world** in a moment of time.

6 And the devil said unto him, **All this power will I give thee, and the glory of them: for that is delivered unto me; and to whomsoever I will I give it.**
KJV

The forces behind these men, worshipped as gods, were really demons and devils. Scripture confirms this:

Deut 32:17-18
17 They sacrificed unto **devils**, not to God; to gods whom they knew not, to new gods that came newly up, whom your fathers feared not.
18 Of the Rock that begat thee thou art unmindful, and hast forgotten God that formed thee.
KJV

These men are themselves representatives of the demons and devils that they serve.

Evil Elves Transformation

In addition, Santa Claus's helpers have their roots in the demon Krampus who accompanied St. Nick and was said to punish bad children in European folklore. Sinterklass, who also brought children gifts, had a helper named Black Pete that punished the children who were bad.

Santa's little helpers are more of a modern invention to make the St. Nicklaus and Sinterklass helpers (Krampus and Black Pete) more economically viable in the age of Christmas being an economic engine. You take a pointy-eared demon Krampus, then shrink, multiply, and change his vocation so he becomes a builder of toys and a helper.

The real source of these helpers may go back to the pagan gods who required children sacrifice in their worship. These children were burned alive in the fire as their parents sacrificed them to their gods. Ancient belief is that the souls of these children would pass through a portal in the fire, where their souls would go and serve these demon gods. This is where the legend of short demons called imps comes from. I know this is shocking but it is confirmed in scripture:

Jer 32:35
35 And they built the high places of Baal, which are in the valley of the son of Hinnom, **to cause their sons and their daughters to pass through the fire unto Molech**; which I commanded them not, neither came it into my mind, that they should do this abomination, to cause Judah to sin.
KJV

Elves come from European folklore for short demons that cause mischief in the woods. There is no doubt that in ancient times these creatures were seen as demons. Whether you believe these myths to be true or not does not change the fact that things thought to be evil were repackaged as good, in the same fashion that Satan was repackaged as Santa. **You can change the package but what is inside is still the same.** It is a common practice of evil to transform the outer package as good yet inside is still pure evil. Apostle Paul expounds on this in scripture:

2 Cor 11:13-15
13 For such are false apostles, deceitful workers, transforming themselves into the apostles of Christ.
14 And **no marvel; for Satan himself is transformed into an angel of light.**
15 Therefore it is no great thing if his ministers also be transformed as the ministers of righteousness; whose end shall be according to their works. (KJV)

Deception

As we have journeyed through the book, we have seen a common theme that Satan works through deception. Sometimes the deception is so complex that it is hard to see, and we need the Holy Spirit to expose the truth. Other times we just have to look closely, and then the deception becomes obvious. Take for example Santa's hat. Do you realize that the very hat is a deception? When you see the truth in it you realize who Santa really is? Pay attention the white ball tip of the hat.

Are you starting to get the picture? Do you realize that the hat is laid to the side so it is not so obvious that it is a pyramid? Still sleep?

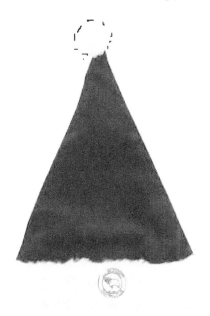

Are you woke yet?

Chapter 11

Excuses for Celebrating

The pagans copied it from us

Many Christians with a lack of knowledge of the Bible and history use this excuse to justify the celebrating of Christmas. This is utterly ridiculous. You have already read the Bible verses, and the early church fathers showing that the world (pagans) were using these same rituals to worship their gods long before it was incorporated into Christianity.

It is ridiculous to say that these pagan rituals that are never mentioned anywhere in the Gospel, originated with Christianity. To think these rituals were stolen by the pagans, with all the proof in the Bible and throughout history (even the testimonies of the early church fathers), is truly putting the cart before the horse. If there is no evidence in the scriptures of God instructing His people in these traditions, then they didn't steal them from us. The truth is we took them from the pagans, which God commanded us, not to do.

It's church tradition

We say Church tradition, but which Church and whose tradition? Is everything that the Church teaches supposed to be accepted as God's will? Are we not supposed to line it up with the Bible first and lean not unto our own understanding? Often I hear people state, "But the Church teaches." The truth be said, the church should be teaching the Bible and if it's not in the Bible or even better yet, if the Bible speaks against it, why is the Church teaching it? Why is it Church tradition?

Col 2:8
8 Beware lest any man spoil you through philosophy and **vain deceit, after the tradition of men, after the rudiments of the world, and not after Christ.**
KJV

What presumption there is to prefer human tradition to divine ordinance! How can we not see that God is indignant angry every time a human tradition relaxes the divine commandments and passes them by. *Cyprian* (c. 250, W), 5.387 DECB pg 647.

We celebrate it in the honor of Christ

Who decides what honors Christ? Are we all free to worship Christ in whatever way we see fit? Are we all free to celebrate Christ in any manner we deem pleasant in our own eyes?

Num 15:38-40
38 Speak unto the children of Israel, and bid them that they make them fringes in the borders of their garments throughout their generations, and that they put upon the fringe of the borders a ribband of blue:
39 And it shall be unto you for a fringe, that ye may look upon it, and remember all the commandments of the LORD, and do them; and that **ye seek not after your own heart and your own eyes, after which ye use to go a whoring:**
40 That ye may remember, and do all my commandments, and be holy unto your God.

Matt 15:9
9 **But in vain they do worship me, teaching for doctrines the commandments of men.**
KJV

If it were wrong, God would have told us by now

Yes, but are you listening?

I don't think God has a problem with it

Nadab and Abihu did not think God had a problem with what they were doing and offered up worship not sanctioned by God.

Lev 10:1-2
10:1 And Nadab and Abihu, the sons of Aaron, took either of them his censer, and put fire therein, and put incense thereon, **and offered strange fire before the LORD, which he commanded them not.**
2 And there went out fire from the LORD, and devoured them, and they died before the LORD.

It won't stop you from getting to heaven

Eph 5:5-17
5 For this ye know, that no whoremonger, nor unclean person, nor covetous man, who is an idolater, hath any inheritance in the kingdom of Christ and of God.
6 Let no man deceive you with vain words: for because of these things cometh the wrath of God upon the children of disobedience.
7 Be not ye therefore partakers with them.
8 For ye were sometimes darkness, but now are ye light in the Lord: walk as children of light:
9(For the fruit of the Spirit is in all goodness and righteousness and truth;)
10 Proving **what is acceptable unto the Lord.**
11 And **have no fellowship with the unfruitful works of darkness, but rather reprove them.**
12 For it is a shame even to speak of those things which are done of them in secret.
13 But all things that are reproved are made manifest by the light: for whatsoever doth make manifest is light.
14 Wherefore he saith, Awake thou that sleepest, and arise from the dead, and Christ shall give thee light.
15 See **then that ye walk circumspectly, not as fools, but as wise,**
16 Redeeming the time, because the days are evil.
17 Wherefore be ye not unwise, but understanding what the will of the Lord is.

You can have a feast day any day as long as it is to honor God!

If this is true, then let me ask you a few questions. Why did you pick December 25th to have your feast day to honor God? Are you following God's instructions, or are you following the world? Did God pick the day or did the world?

Israel decided to have a feast in honor of Yahweh (God), and they named the calf that they made Yahweh. People do not realize that in Hebrew the name translated "God" was "Yahweh" meaning it was in honor of the true God. Aaron the high priest of Israel sanctioned the feast to Yahweh. God brought judgment down on the people because what they were doing in the worship of Him was not sanctioned by Him.

Ex 32:4-5
4 And he received them at their hand, and fashioned it with a graving tool, after he had made it a molten calf: and they said, These be thy gods, O Israel, which brought thee up out of the land of Egypt.
5 And when Aaron saw it, he built an altar before it; and Aaron made proclamation, and said, To morrow is a feast to the LORD.

Israel named a calf Yahweh taking an image from Egypt to worship God. People who have read the Bible already know how the story ended. Didn't turn out too good, did it?

Deut 12:32
32 **What thing soever I command you, observe to do it: thou shalt not add thereto, nor diminish from it.**
KJV

DOES THE WORLD ACCEPT THE THINGS OF GOD? NO!! Strangely yet, they do accept Christmas but not Christ!

John 7:3-7
3 His brethren therefore said unto him, Depart hence, and go into Judaea, that thy disciples also may see the works that thou doest.

4 For there is no man that doeth any thing in secret, and he himself seeketh to be known openly. If thou do these things, shew thyself to the world.

5 For neither did his brethren believe in him.

6 Then Jesus said unto them, My time is not yet come: but your time is alway ready.

7 **The world cannot hate you; but me it hateth, because I testify of it, that the works thereof are evil.**

The Saturnalia, New Year, Midwinter festivals, and Matronalia are frequented by us! Presents come and go! There are New Years gifts! Games join their noise! Banquets join their din! The pagans are more faithful to their own sect.... For, even if they had known them, they would not have shared the Lord's Day or Pentecost with us. For they would fear least they would appear to be Christians. Yet, we are not apprehensive that we might appear to be pagans! *Tertullian* (c. 200, W), 3.70 DECB pg 342

Why do we accept the things of the world?

1 John 2:14-17

14 I have written unto you, fathers, because ye have known him that is from the beginning. I have written unto you, young men, because ye are strong, and the word of God abideth in you, and ye have overcome the wicked one.

15 **Love not the world, neither the things that are in the world. If any man love the world, the love of the Father is not in him.**

16 For all that is in the world, the lust of the flesh, and the lust of the eyes, and the pride of life, is not of the Father, but is of the world.

17 And the world passeth away, and the lust thereof: but he that doeth the will of God abideth for ever.

This world and the next are two enemies.... We cannot therefore be friends of both. *Second Clement* (c. 150), 7.518 DECB pg 697

So long as you deem yourself a Christian, you are a different man from a pagan. Give him back his own views of things! After all, he does not himself learn from your views. Why lean upon a blind guide, If you have eyes of your own? Why be clothed by one that is naked, if you have put on Christ? *Tertullian* (c. 210, W), 3.547 DECB pg 698

WHAT GOD IS SAYING

Prov 19:20-21
20 Hear counsel, and receive instruction, that thou mayest be wise in thy latter end.
21 There are many devices in a man's heart; nevertheless the counsel of the **LORD,** that shall stand.

Wake up! Stand upright, People of God.

Chapter 12

In Remembrance of Me

Luke 22:19-20
19 And he took bread, and gave thanks, and brake it, and gave unto them, saying, This is my body which is given for you: this do in remembrance of me.
20 Likewise also the cup after supper, saying, This cup is the new testament in my blood, which is shed for you.
KJV

Why is it that the majority of the world has never read these verses? Why is it that most people who identify themselves as Christians are not aware that these verses contain the only thing that Christ commanded the believers to do in remembrance of Him? Today we call it communion and most Christians who have gone to church on a regular basis have participated in this Christian ritual commanded by Christ. So why hasn't the world embraced this? Why haven't you seen items for communion in the malls even at Christmas time? Why haven't you seen commercials selling items for communion? Why is there no mention of these sacraments in anyway for any holiday? **Do we really understand that this is the one and only thing that Christ said, "Do in remembrance of me"?** So why does the world reject it? Because unlike Christmas it really is of God, so they cannot embrace it. The world wants nothing to do with the Light of this world. They want nothing to do with Christ. That alone should make us understand Christmas.

John 17:14
14 I have given them thy word; and the world hath hated them, because they are not of the world, even as I am not of the world. KJV

I had a friend and a co-worker who is an evangelist in the Body of Christ. She was one of the brethren that told me I needed to be careful in speaking against Christmas because she believed that to speak against it was to spread false doctrines. I took it personally because this sister in Christ had a hand in mentoring me as a babe in Christ. She is a real woman of God and loves the Lord. I knew what God was showing me was supported by scripture, but the Christmas ideology is so embedded in people that it is like pulling teeth to speak against it. It is hard to uproot false teachings that are bound up in emotional memories. Very few people accept this word initially, but God always waters the seed of His Word. I have been shocked over the years at the amount of people I have spoken to who have come back to me with testimonies of how God watered His Word and allowed them to embrace His truth.

Months after the evangelist rejected what God had revealed to me about Christmas, she came back and said she had to share a testimony with me. She told me she was sitting on her couch watching the Macy's Christmas parade, and all of a sudden, God spoke to her. He said, "Why is it that the world will not accept anything of me?" She shared that she jumped up and said, "Because you are holy and righteous and they don't want anything to do with you." She started crying and glorifying God, praising His name and ended on her knees sobbing. She heard nothing else and she finally got up and sat back down on the couch. She continued watching the Macy's Christmas parade, but God was not finished. He spoke one more sentence to her and as she repeated it to me, the magnitude of the words almost knocked me off my feet. He said, "Then why do they accept Christmas?" She said she started balling. She finally got it. They accept Christmas because it is not of God. All over the world in almost every nation, you see Christmas trees, lights, wreaths on doors, and presents being exchanged. I have been shocked at how many other religions have some type of Christmas celebration. Even atheists will be reveling at Christmas parties filled with the Christmas spirit with a Christmas tree standing in some corner of the building. Most of the world is celebrating on Christmas day. Yet, God's truth is riveting. The world will not accept anything of Him, and the only reason they accept Christmas is that the spirits, in charge of this present world, know it has nothing to do with the true and only God.

I want to leave you with a personal testimony. It was the year 2000 on a Wednesday night in early December. I was feeling cheerful because I was entering church for Bible study. It was always good to be around fellow Christians, and I was looking forward to the fellowship. I entered the church through the quad doors at the northern entrance by the altar. I walked by it and didn't even notice. I made a sharp right turn in the middle section of the pews where the congregation sat for Bible study. Pleasant faces greeted me as I walked back to sit on a bench that was empty. As I sat down, I bowed my head and said a short prayer. I lifted up my head and gazed around the church just to take in the scenery. I gasped not believing what I was seeing.

Many years before, I had promised myself that I would not sit in a church to worship where there was a Christmas tree. It did not matter that the church was oblivious to what the scripture said about placing a tree by the altar of God. I knew the truth. I knew what God said. As I sat there in disbelief, I contemplated what to do. It would not look right for me to get up and walk out after I had just walked in. I sat staring at the tree. It did not even look good; it was dark and had the appearance of a tree meant to be placed in the deep woods. I did not even notice at the time that it was sitting in the same position where God had pointed out the image of jealousy to Ezekiel at the north entrance by the altar of the temple. What was I going to do?

I knew what I had to do. It is better to comply with God's will than to go against God to not offend others. The others might have been ignorant of the meaning of the tree, but I was not. I grabbed my Bible, got up, and walked out the same door that I came in through. I could see the eyes looking at me perplexed as to why I was leaving. I was upset. My train of thought was, "They should know." I was still a babe in Christ, and if I understood that God commanded that no trees be placed by His altar, how could the church not know? I was so upset my eyes were watering. I got in my car and drove out of the church parking lot. That is when I heard clear as day, **"They have not rejected you, they have rejected me."** It caught me by surprise that God was there all the time watching. He sees everything, and even though I was upset, He had more right to be upset because to reject His Word is to reject Him. It would be years later before I realized that what He said to me was actually a quote from the Bible.

Imagine my surprise when I found the quote in scripture and realized God spoke the very words to Samuel who is my namesake. Yet, even then, I did not realize that the words spoken were at the exact time that the nation of Israel stopped walking upright before God and became a beast nation. At Gilgal, He hated them just as He hates when His people today throw out the Word of God so we can keep our traditions. Christ emphasized this point many times in His ministry:

Mark 7:9
9 And he said unto them, **Full well ye reject the commandment of God, that ye may keep your own tradition.**
KJV

I could have sat there that day not wanting to offend and waited until after the service to leave, but I wonder if God would have still spoken to me after I compromised. I do not think so. I finally understand that because I could not compromise the truth, God revealed with His Word that He was taking me to a deeper place of understanding. God quoted the scripture that told the whole story of how His people rejected Him so they could be like the world. **When we walk according to God's truth, He takes us deeper. When we stand for God, He will let it be known that He is standing with us.** Joseph, Daniel, David, and many more men and women of God prove that when you stand with God, He stands with you. He was letting me know that He was with me.

Our God is not dead, He is alive. He is with us. When we walk upright before Him, He manifests in our lives to let us know He is with us. The Body of Christ is not a beast. It is a congregation of those in Christ with the Son of God as our head. We are in Him because we not only believe but also obey Him. Christ is with His church. One day we will all sit with Him at the wedding feast and participate in the heavenly Passover. He will take the heavenly bread, give it to each and everyone of us, and say, "This is my body broken for you." He will then pass us the gold cup with heavenly wine and say, "This cup is the New Testament in my blood, which is shed for you."

Every time we do this ritual (right hand) in remembrance of the sacrifice he made (forehead), we not only point back to what He did, we also point forward to where we will be.

Rev 15:2-4
2 And **I saw as it were a sea of glass mingled with fire: and them that had gotten the victory over the beast, and over his image, and over his mark, and over the number of his name, stand on the sea of glass, having the harps of God.**
3 And they sing the song of Moses the servant of God, and the song of the Lamb, saying, Great and marvellous are thy works, Lord God Almighty; just and true are thy ways, thou King of saints.
4 Who shall not fear thee, O Lord, and glorify thy name? for thou only art holy: for all nations shall come and worship before thee; for thy judgments are made manifest.
KJV

Thank you for taking this journey with me, it has really been a pleasure.

Num 6:24-26
**24 The LORD bless thee, and keep thee:
25 The LORD make his face shine upon thee, and be gracious unto thee:
26 The LORD lift up his countenance upon thee, and give thee peace.
KJV**

The Need for Salvation

If you are reading (or have read) this book and you do not know Christ Jesus as your personal Savior, all it takes is a simple prayer to change your circumstance and start you on the pathway to eternal life. Christ came and died in your place to save you from sin and eternal damnation. Do you understand why His death was necessary? God did not create the world to be wicked and to perish, but He did give all humanity freewill. When Adam sinned in disobeying God, it allowed wickedness to enter the world through sin. God has appointed a day to judge the wickedness of this world.

God loves the creation He has made. He sent his Son Jesus (Yehoshua) to redeem the earth and all those who believe (accept Christ and walk in His truth) that God sent His Son to die so that we all might live.

Christ's death and resurrection from the dead enables us to come back into relationship with the Father. He took the penalty of death for us to remove our sins, and bring us back into a right relationship with God. With a right relationship comes the renewal of our spirit, which allows us to sense and understand spiritual things. His resurrection represents our spiritual renewing and the hope of eternal life in God's Kingdom.

(Precious Bible Promises)

YOU ARE A SINNER...
Rom 3:10
10 As it is written, There is none righteous, no, not one:

1 John 1:8
8 If we say that we have no sin, we deceive ourselves, and the truth is not in us.

Rom 3:23
23 For all have sinned, and come short of the glory of God;

THERE IS A PRICE TO BE PAID FOR SIN...
Eph 5:3-7
3 But fornication, and all uncleanness, or covetousness, let it not be once named among you, as becometh saints;
4 Neither filthiness, nor foolish talking, nor jesting, which are not convenient: but rather giving of thanks.
5 For this ye know, that no whoremonger, nor unclean person, nor covetous man, who is an idolater, hath any inheritance in the kingdom of Christ and of God.
6 Let no man deceive you with vain words: for because of these things cometh the wrath of God upon the children of disobedience.
7 Be not ye therefore partakers with them.

Gal 5:19-21
19 Now the works of the flesh are manifest, which are these; Adultery, fornication, uncleanness, lasciviousness,
20 Idolatry, witchcraft, hatred, variance, emulations, wrath, strife, seditions, heresies,
21 Envyings, murders, drunkenness, revellings, and such like: of the which I tell you before, as I have also told you in time past, that they which do such things shall not inherit the kingdom of God.

1 Cor 6:9-10
9 Know ye not that the unrighteous shall not inherit the kingdom of God? Be not deceived: neither fornicators, nor idolaters, nor adulterers, nor effeminate, nor abusers of themselves with mankind,
10 Nor thieves, nor covetous, nor drunkards, nor revilers, nor extortioners, shall inherit the kingdom of God.

GOD TAKES NO PLEASURE IN ANYONE GOING TO HELL...
Ezek 33:11
11 Say unto them, As I live, saith the Lord GOD, I have no pleasure in the death of the wicked; but that the wicked turn from his way and live: turn ye, turn ye from your evil ways; for why will ye die, O house of Israel?

1 Tim 2:4
4 Who will have all men to be saved, and to come unto the knowledge of the truth.

NEED OF REPENTANCE...
2 Peter 3:9
9 The Lord is not slack concerning his promise, as some men count slackness; but is longsuffering to us-ward, not willing that any should perish, but that all should come to repentance.

Luke 5:32
32 I came not to call the righteous, but sinners to repentance.

Acts 3:19
19 Repent ye therefore, and be converted, that your sins may be blotted out, when the times of refreshing shall come from the presence of the Lord;

GOD LOVES YOU...
Rev 3:19-20
19 As many as I love, I rebuke and chasten: be zealous therefore, and repent.
20 Behold, I stand at the door, and knock: if any man hear my voice, and open the door, I will come in to him, and will sup with him, and he with me.

GOD SENT HIS SON JESUS TO SAVE YOU...
Matt 18:11
11 For the Son of man is come to save that which was lost.

John 3:16-18
16 For God so loved the world, that he gave his only begotten Son, that whosoever believeth in him should not perish, but have everlasting life.
17 For God sent not his Son into the world to condemn the world; but that the world through him might be saved.
18 He that believeth on him is not condemned: but he that believeth not is condemned already, because he hath not believed in the name of the only begotten Son of God.

CHRIST DIED FOR YOU AND WANTS TO SAVE YOU...
Rom 6:23
23 For the wages of sin is death; but the gift of God is eternal life through Jesus Christ our Lord.

Rom 5:6-8

6 For when we were yet without strength, in due time Christ died for the ungodly.

7 For scarcely for a righteous man will one die: yet peradventure for a good man some would even dare to die.

8 But God commendeth his love toward us, in that, while we were yet sinners, Christ died for us.

CHRIST CAN SAVE YOU NOW...

Rom 10:9-10

9 That if thou shalt confess with thy mouth the Lord Jesus, and shalt believe in thine heart that God hath raised him from the dead, thou shalt be saved.

10 For with the heart man believeth unto righteousness; and with the mouth confession is made unto salvation.

YOU CAN KNOW THAT YOU'RE SAVED...

1 John 5:10-13

10 He that believeth on the Son of God hath the witness in himself: he that believeth not God hath made him a liar; because he believeth not the record that God gave of his Son.

11 And this is the record, that God hath given to us eternal life, and this life is in his Son.

12 He that hath the Son hath life; and he that hath not the Son of God hath not life.

13 These things have I written unto you that believe on the name of the Son of God; that ye may know that ye have eternal life, and that ye may believe on the name of the Son of God.

A Sinner's Prayer...

Father, the Creator of all things, I come to You today and confess that I am a sinner. I confess that I believe that You sent your Son Christ Jesus to die for my sins to bring me back into relationship with You. I accept what He has done and repent for all my past sins. (Confess all pass sins that you can remember.) Forgive me Father, renew my spirit, and lead me in the way of righteousness. I ask this in the name of your Son Jesus Christ. AMEN!

Maranatha!

References

Fausset's Bible Dictionary, Electronic Database Copyright (c)1998, 2003 by Biblesoft

International Standard Bible Encyclopaedia, Electronic Database Copyright © 1996, 2003 by Biblesoft, Inc. All rights reserved.)

Precious Bible Promises (From the New King James Version) (c) 1983 Thomas Nelson, Publishers.

David W. Bercot, Editor A Dictionary of Early Christian Beliefs. Peabody, Hendrickson Publisher, Inc. 1998

Paul L. Maier Eusebius-- The Church History Grand Rapids: Kregel Publications, 1999

Williams Samuel, The Truth about the Tithe Copyright (c) 2016

Williams Samuel, Assault on Innocence Copyright (c) 2017

Other Books by this Author

Witchcraft In The Church (Exposing the Enemies' Infiltration)
Sleep Paralysis
Prayer - A Deeper Understanding
Hidden In The Garden
Assault On Innocence (Protecting the Children)
Hidden In The Metaphor (Excerpt from "Hidden In The Garden")
The Armor of God (Excerpt from "Assault On Innocence")
The Truth about the Tithe (Making Merchandise of God's People)
Curses and Tithes, Truth and Lies (Excerpt from "The Truth About the Tithes")

Note from the Author

Let Others Know!
If this book has been a blessing to you, please share the good news by visiting Amazon.com and leaving a positive review.
Your review is greatly appreciated. Thank you!
Let's Stay Connected!
If you would like to be placed on a contact list to be notified of future books, please email me at Samuelkem@aol.com.
Type "**Book Contact List**" in the subject line and **include your name and email address in the email** itself. Thank you!

References

Made in the USA
Coppell, TX
20 May 2022

77996276R00095